NATIVE AMERICAN YOUTH
AND ALCOHOL

NATIVE AMERICAN YOUTH AND ALCOHOL

An Annotated Bibliography

MICHAEL L. LOBB
and
THOMAS D. WATTS

Foreword by Russell D. Mason

Bibliographies and Indexes in Sociology, Number 16

GREENWOOD PRESS
New York • Westport, Connecticut • London

Dedicated with love to
my grandmother, Sarrilda Gambol Lyle Lobb
and
to my daughter, Rebecca Anne Watts

Library of Congress Cataloging-in-Publication Data

Lobb, Michael L., 1942-
    Native American youth and alcohol : an annotated bibliography /
Michael L. Lobb and Thomas D. Watts ; foreword by Russell D. Mason.
        p.   cm.—(Bibliographies and indexes in sociology, ISSN
0742-6895 ; no. 16)
    Includes index.
    ISBN 0-313-25618-7 (lib. bdg. : alk. paper)
        1. Indians of North America—Alcohol use—Bibliography.
2. Indians of North America—Youth—Bibliography. I. Watts, Thomas
D. II. Title. III. Series.
Z1209.2.U5L6   1989
[E98.L7]
016.3622'92'08997—dc19   88-32345

British Library Cataloguing in Publication Data is available.

Library of Congress Catalog Card Number: 88-32345
ISBN: 0-313-25618-7
ISSN: 0742-6895

First published in 1989

Greenwood Press, Inc.
88 Post Road West, Westport, Connecticut 06881

Printed in the United States of America

The paper used in this book complies with the
Permanent Paper Standard issued by the National
Information Standards Organization (Z39.48-1984).

10 9 8 7 6 5 4 3 2 1

CONTENTS

FOREWORD

On October 27, 1986, President Reagan signed into law
Public Law 99-570. Subtitle C of the Law entitled
"Indian Alcohol and Substance Abuse Prevention and
Treatment Act of 1986" calls for a comprehensive, coordinated attack upon the severe alcoholism and
substance abuse problem in American Indian/Alaska
Native communities. Also, it addresses Indian youth
programs, focusing on treatment centers and preventive
intervention school-based program activities.

American Indians/Alaska Natives between the ages
of 15 and 24 years are more than two times as likely to
commit suicide as the general population and
approximately 80 percent of those suicides are
alcohol-related. In addition, American Indian/Alaska
Native youths between the ages of 15 and 24 years are
twice as likely as the general population to die in
automobile accidents, 75 percent of which are alcohol-
related.

This timely annotated bibliography makes a most
valuable contribution by emphasizing the current and
relevant publications on Indian youth and alcohol.
This book will have utility throughout the human
services field, especially among researchers,
practitioners, tribal leaders, and those who are
currently involved in health promotion and disease
prevention activities.

Russell D. Mason
Chief, Alcoholism and Substance
  Abuse Program Branch
Indian Health Service
Rockville, Maryland

INTRODUCTION
AND
REVIEW OF THE
LITERATURE

A literature or body of scholarly works is known by its issues and authors. Just as authors can develop with experience and achieve identity through maturity, so also can issues achieve definition as researchers contribute to the collective body of knowledge. When several well defined issues are observed to be associated conceptually or to arise from a common data base, the collected works are referred to as " a literature," as for example, the literature on alcoholism. The literature on Native American youth alcoholism is in its infancy. Although at a juvenile stage, this literature has achieved recognition as a common body of collected knowledge having not only traditional issues with roots in anthropology, sociology, but also specific issues unique to Native American youth alcoholism such as child abuse and neglect, foster homes, school problems, dropouts, peer relation effects, family modeling response, fetal alcohol syndrome, prevention, sniffing, developmental factors, cohort methodology, and rural versus urban factors as well as others. Thus, it seems appropriate to acknowledge by reviewing this literature that Native American youth alcoholism is coming of age.

Any review of the Native American alcohol literature must begin by recognizing the keystone annotated bibliography by Mail and McDonald containing the definitive literature review by Leland. We see this literature as a collection of works primarily anchored in anthropology and identified by issues such as suicide, consumption rate, cross cultural effects, methodologies, the need to debunk, treatment, youth, health, and social deprivation. The emerging literature on Native American youth alcoholism is more multidisciplinary in nature, perhaps suggesting that the Native American alcohol literature in general has attracted more attention from various disciplines since the 1980 publication by Mail and McDonald. The catalog

of issues in Native American youth alcohol diverges
from that list by Mail and McDonald as indicated above.
Furthermore, many of the proposed relationships are
questioned as subsequent research has been published,
but other issues and proposed relations have survived
the scrutiny of systematic research.   Social
deprivation, for example, has a well documented,
prominent effect on alcohol consumption in any peoples
of any age or ethnic background where alcohol is
readily available.   But among Native American youth,
this issue takes on special significance as in general,
it promotes developmental delays, and in specific, is
more common to Native American youth with its attendant
rural/social isolation, sensory deprivation and
cultural assimilation crisis.   The Native American
youth is, simply put, more at risk of social
deprivation effects.

Since Mail and McDonald published their work,
several other issues have been defied as having a
particular and significant relevance to Native American
youth alcoholism.   We will review these as well as
catalog the issues having historical roots in sociology
and anthropology, per se.   In general, we pursue the
published work of any and all disciplines having
relevance for Native American youth alcoholism.

ACCIDENTAL DEATH

Death from accidents is the second leading cause of death among Native Americans, while it is the fourth leading cause for the total population. Indeed, in 1979 the age-adjusted accident death rate of the Native American population was over three times that of the population as a whole (Health Resources and Services Administration, 1985: 139). Hence it is surprising that there is a sparsity of related literature on accidental death in Native American youth alcoholism. The limited literature that does exist deals mostly with the identification and treatment of drinking as it is related to accidental death, and only in a minor way is this then related to Native American youth. Principally, this literature calls for the development of psychometric tests to identify the problem drinker and for the design of treatment programs. Numerous important research questions have not been explored in this literature, which is ripe for further research. Impulse control among Native American youth is one of the significant factors that has not been studied. Furthermore, suicide-motivated accidental death in this group is neither studied nor reported in the literature. There would also be an increased opportunity to drink as a result of escaping structure and restrictions, through driving, and this has not been studied in Native American youths, nor has the increased physical access through driving been studied. The exposure to drunken drivers as a result of dating is unstudied, and this appears to be particularly significant as male Native American youths are far more likely to drink than females, and thus females may be exposed to accidental death through the inebriation of their dates.

There is also a need to study the advisability to include driving restrictions in treatment programs, and in all of this literature there is an absence of reports of accidents not involving driving, such as lethal consumption levels, operating other heavy machinery, drug interactions, and so on. Basically, this remains a significantly under-studied area of considerable importance.

BIOMEDICAL FACTORS

The major issues that arise in the literature on biomedical factors in Native American youth alcoholism are principally genetic factors, factors of associated diseases, and the literature on fetal alcohol syndrome (FAS). Fetal alcohol syndrome has several important subissues, including risk factors, education, prevention, treatment, and diagnosis.

The standard criteria for diagnosis of fetal alcohol syndrome (Smith, 1981) includes delayed development, characteristic facial appearances, maternal alcoholism, and poor growth. To these Smith adds significant skeletal findings, including cervical spine fusion, abnormal thoracic cage development, delayed bone age, and cardiac lesions including functional murmurs. This is supported by the United States Indian Health Service report on an outline of training curriculum for fetal alcohol syndrome in which they indicate that clinical aspects of FAS include central nervous system damage and physical abnormalities. The central nervous system damage is further identified by McShane and Willenbring (1984) in which they identify changes in neuronal densities as a function of alcohol abuse independent of ethnicity. Using CAT scan technology, these authors confirm ethnic differences in asymmetry patterns in the occipital lobes, particularly relating to length and width within the lobe. However, above the base rate for ethnic differences in neuronal densities and asymmetry, they find significant differences for alcohol abuse. Johnson (1979) further expands the list of FAS to include rhinorrhea, otitis media, choanal stenosis, and hypoplastic ethmoid. Garver (1982) reports on the corneal curvature differences in FAS children. He finds the average horizontal curvature to be significantly steeper in this group. Risk factors have also been identified in fetal alcohol syndrome, and Aase in his paper on fetal alcohol syndrome in American Indians reports risk factors to include cultural influences, fertility, patterns of alcohol consumption and abuse, and even dietary and metabolic differences. In a subsequent study, he also finds zinc deficiency to be associated with the disease. Thus the literature on fetal alcohol syndrome in this group has recently undergone an expanded diagnostic criteria. Perhaps the most definitive bibliographies on the subject are those by Abel (1986) and the United States Indian Health Service entitled "Bibliography on Fetal Alcohol Syndrome and Related Issues"(1981). The more recent literature has tended to further define.

the disorder and its associated features. The prevailing consensus is that a working definition exists and that the research area is under active development.

The issue of education and treatment for fetal alcohol syndrome is pursued by numerous authors including the California Urban Indian Health Council (1981) who proposed that the identity of Indian women of child-bearing age who appear to have drinking problems is the first priority in beginning an education program. Hynbaugh (1983) proposes a flexible multidisciplinary approach to the treatment of FAS and New Breast (1976) proposes targeting the mothers as the high risk factor for prevention and treatment.

The genetic factors in fetal alcohol syndrome have basically followed the historical argument that there are genetic differences in alcohol dehydrogenase and aldehyde dehydrogenase among America Indians versus non-American Indians. This has presumed on the hypothesis that the ethnic origin of the American Indian is to be found on the Asian continent where alcohol dehydrogenase is known to be a significant factor in intoxication. The synopsis of the recent literature on this point, however, does not support the hypothesis. Rex, Boyron, Smialek, and Li (1985) report on the study of alcohol dehydrogenase and aldehyde dehydrogenase in New Mexico Native Americans. They find that the frequency of the aldehyde dehydrogenase allele was .59 and was far higher than any other ratio for population. There results show that both alcohol dehydrogenase and aldehyde dehydrogenase phenotypes among American Indians are more like those of the Caucasian population and significantly different from those of the Oriental population. Schuckit (1980) finds that even among people who have the phenotypic alleles and are genetically predisposed, the clinical picture of alcoholism involves a combination of genetic and environmental factors. Basically, this takes the approach of expressivity modifiers in determining the outcome of the disorder. The genetic hypothesis for a predisposition toward alcoholism is also not supported by the findings of Goedde et al (1983), who found that their evidence confirms that the aldehyde dehydrogenase isozyme deficiency and implied alcohol sensitivity exist in Orientals but not in South American Indians. Finally, Zeiner (   ) in his paper on drug dependency and alcoholism finds that the physiological reactions to alcohol include facial flushing, tachycardia, decreased blood pressure, increased skin conductants, and are more idiosyncratic than genetically based within a group.

Thus, in conclusion, the hypothesis of an ethnic predisposition on genetic basis is not supported by the data. In general, genetic predispositions, even of a recessive nature, would require expressivity modifiers in the form of cultural and environmental influences to bring the alcoholism to a problematic level. This has considerable significance for policy and prevention as in effect it says that the genetic basis is not the preeminent factor and that significant emphasis should be put on cultural and environmental remediation.

Numerous diseases are associated with alcohol abuse. Baxter et al. (1986) report middle ear infection to be significantly higher among this group of Native American youth abusing alcohol. Meningococcal disease has been found in numerous Native American youth populations abusing alcohol. Counts et al. (1984) report that nearly one-half of the people with meningococcal disease were Native Americans and two-thirds were alcohol abusers. Outbreaks of the disease among the group have also been reported by Middaugh (1981). The skid-row community was found to be a significant factor in predicting the occurrence of the disease. In all reports, the disease is effectively treated through vaccination. Reyes de la Rocha, Brown and Fortenbury (1987) report on reduced lung volume following spray paint inhalation for an average of thirty-five months, three times per week. Pulmonary testing also included airway resistance and airway conductants that were affected negatively by this experience. The use of a bronchodilator had positive results in remediating this presenting problem. Finally, Hoy, Megill, and Hughson (1987) report on renal failure among Zuni Indians having an unknown cause. This disorder was suggested to be of epidemic proportions, and one-third of the cases were estimated to be caused by two types of diabetes. Exposure to toxic substances, which can include alcohol, were suggested in the analysis of causative factors.

In conclusion, biomedical factors are principally vested in genetic associated diseases and FAS topics within the literature. Other areas have not yet been sufficiently defined to warrant treatment as a separate topic. Perhaps the most significant topic for policies and programs arises out of the genetic studies while associated diseases and the fetal alcohol data have more significance for immediate treatment research.

CRIME

The major topic areas identified through a review of the literature on crime are criminal justice, child abuse and neglect, delinquency, and the theories on the antecedents of crime. Stewart (1964) was the first to draw meaningful comparisons between Native American and total population arrests, and subsequently, several prominent hypotheses have been put forth by others to explain the occurrence of crime among American Indian youths. There is a significant controversy between Lewellyn (1981) with his hypoglycemia-induced aggression hypotheses versus Bolton's (1984) and other papers arguing that hypoglycemia is not the antecedent but that alcohol disinhibition of aggression is the most valid hypothesis. Clearly, the data are not sufficient to preclude one hypothesis over the other, and on balance multiple causality has to be considered. Wolfe (1984) suggests that violence among American Indians is related to the alcohol blackout syndrome which includes damage to the medial thalamus, hypothalamus, and red nucleus. Destruction of nuclei in these areas results in a loss of conscious cortical control over emotion and, by implication, the ability to withhold aggression. Wolfe reports data suggesting that the development of this syndrome is more rapid in American Indians than in non-American Indians, and that it occurs earlier in their drinking history. Olson, Carman, and Pasewark (1978) propose that population density increases liquor sales while liquor sales increases the incidence of public intoxication and DWI. This is sociological correlative data, but nonetheless, is suggestive of causal relationships between the indicated factors. Similar correlative data is also coming in support of alcoholism in conjunction with homicides from a sociological standpoint. For example, Bloom (1980) reports that alcoholism is the most frequent diagnosis among homicide-indicted American Indians. Jilek and Chunila (1979) report that American Indian homicide rates are three times that of Anglos of comparable ages. Alcohol abuse is a prominent factor in their data, although they do not postulate a cause and effect relationship. They do, however, point out that Native Indians are overrepresented for manslaughter indictments.

Similar theories have been put forth to account for juvenile delinquency. Underhill (1970) proposes that juvenile delinquency is caused by cultural conflict, expectation of failure, unemployment, failures of parents, inadequate education, and most notably, alcoholism.

The United States Indian Health Service in its 1970 report on the Reno/Sparks Indian Colony relates absenteeism, delinquency, and low achievement to early educational termination or dropout. They deny a relationship between juvenile delinquency and population density, family stability, or socioeconomic status. Finally, Marshall, Kaplin, Gans, and Kahn (1969) argue that social disorganization is a principal cause of delinquency among American Indian youths. Their view of social disorganization is that it is an insidious variable brought about by inadequate, misdirected, and unresponsive public administration. They argue that social disorganization is a principal antecedent to crime.

Schaefer (1973) reports that more American Indian than non-American Indian adolescents are arrested or are prone to police encounters owing to alcohol related incidents. He argues that the principal factor is public rather than private consumption, with public consumption producing greater visibility. He argues that this is a greater and more significant factor than low socioeconomic status.

The information on child abuse and neglect is surprisingly low in frequency of reports considering the considerable discussion and dialogue that went on in the development of the Indian Child Welfare Act. However, among those few extant reports, there are some significant indications for child abuse and neglect in American Indian youths as this is related to alcoholism. Fischler (1985) reports that child abuse and neglect in American Indians is equal to that in non-American Indians. He reports that there is insufficient data to define the American Indian child abuse and neglect profile. However, there are several significant factors in the promulgation of child abuse and neglect, including cultural misunderstanding, modernization, poverty, situational stress, poor parenting skills, and alcoholism. He rejects removal of children from families as treatment. Long (1986) reports four case studies of violent crime including rape of children which are reported to be alcohol-related. In conclusion, it is surprising to find the low frequency of alcohol-related child abuse and neglect reports considering the significant implication of this factor in alcoholism studies in non-American Indians. There is a clear need for more data in this area.

The data on delinquency are similarly limited. Forslund (1974) reports that although American Indians have higher reported incidences of delinquency than Anglos, a questionnaire issued among adolescents of both groups indicated no

significant differences in self-report. The suggestion
here is that the true incidences of delinquent
behaviors are equal among the ethnic groups but
that the American Indians are more prone to be
identified. This is consistent with Schaefer's
(1973) hypothesis of public versus private
consumption as being a major factor of being
identified. Forslund also reports that American
Indian females are more likely to run away than
non-American Indian females, and that American
Indians have higher drug uses than Anglos. Forslund
reports that all differences can be accounted for by
low socioeconomic status (SES).

In a subsequent 1974 paper, Forslund also argues
that American Indian delinquency is greater than
Anglo delinquency, and that American Indians are more
prone to report the delinquency related to alcohol
and minor offenses, and again argues for the SES
implication. The United States Indian Health Service
report of 1970 on the Reno/Sparks Indian Colony as
indicated above, relates the problem to early
educational termination. However, Phillips and Inui
(1986) argue that higher educational achievement and
residential status in larger communities are more
likely to be associated with greater psychosocial
maladjustment.

Finally, there is a significant theme within the
literature on the criminal justice system. The
United States Bureau of Indian Affairs report of 1972
carries considerable nationwide statistics on crime
among Indians reported by Indian law enforcement
agencies. They use the same index as the FBI, and
report a full range and frequency of criminal behavior.
These include offenses involving intoxication, liquor,
and drugs. A similar report from the United States
Bureau of Indian Affairs (1976) also reports the
statistics in aggregate. Both of these reports are
far too extensive to be paraphrased here. Gilbert
(1985) reports on the need for alcohol training as a
priority among American Indian police owing to the
high prevalence of alcohol-related crimes. Harrell
(1981) reports on the factor of remorse in
alcohol-related crimes as it impacts sentencing. He
notes that remorse with an alcoholism history reduces
the sentencing for minor offences but increases the
sentencing for major offenses among American Indian
youth. This may implicate an escape strategy,
learned by environmental system cues in which minor
crimes are overlooked due to remorse and
alcoholism, which in turn leads the perpetrator
to the erroneous expectation that major crimes can be
similarly overlooked. Thus the system may be
sending an incorrect signal to the recipients of
the criminal justice system. Finally, Stewart

ETIOLOGY

The literature on the etiology of Native American youth alcoholism is not sufficiently developed to warrant subheadings nor is it sufficient to identification of specific themes within the literature. In order for a specific or unique theme to have been developed, more than four authors are needed to have published in the same area. This general area deals with the causality on an antecedent side of alcoholism behavior in this risk group.

The Alaskan Native Health Board in 1970 published the results of a survey of subjective assessment of Native American youth alcohol factors in determining predispositions toward alcoholic behaviors. They subsequently followed up in 1976 with a survey of Native American students and found no differences in grief, isolation, reading disabilities, learning disabilities, home-sickness, negative feelings, and boredom in differentiating between slight and moderate to severe alcohol abusers. Only the factor of boredom appeared to separate these two risk groups. Boredom was also reported along with anger and frustration as factors that impact the causation and predisposition toward drinking by the United States Indian Health Service (1969). Compulsiveness has been studied also as a causative factor, as reported by Couture (1981). Couture reports on a social/cultural approach to identifying positive factors and cites compulsiveness as a significant factor in the results of that study. Sniffing behavior has been frequently sited as a causative factor, as for example, Richard (1981) relates indirectly sniffing and familial factors in Native American youth alcoholism. Albaugh and Albaugh (1979) report that chronic sniffing is a precursory behavior to alcoholic behaviors and that the predisposing factors are reported to include family dynamics, emotional deprivation, and family alcoholism role models. This theme of family transmission of alcoholism predispositions is also reported by Jones-Saumty, Hochgas, Dru, and Zeines, (1983) who studied family factors and alcohol transmission among Native American youth.

Cultural difference arguments have frequently been found in the etiology literature as it has been found throughout the reviews in this book. Kearns (1981) reports a methodological comment on cultural differences between researchers and subjects in determining outcomes and conclusions. Gomberg (1982) argues for the importance of identifying causative factors by age, sex, and ethnicity. He provides a summary of the special drinking problems of Native

American youth by culture. Estes, Smith-Di Julio, and Heinemann (1980) studied the causative factors in Native American youth cross cultures, as did Barbor (1986) who reports an extensive review of causative factors including national, cultural, and individual behavior patterns causative to drinking.

Lewis (1982) examined the unique relationship between the federal government and Native Americans in the etiology of their alcoholism, and Thomas (1981) issued a report that has implications for culturally based etiology of Native American youth alcoholism. Finally, the United States Indian Health Service (1979) published a compendium of statistics on Native American alcoholism including youth alcoholism etiology factors. One such factor is low socioeconomic status, and the United States Indian Health Service (1972) reports that low socioeconomic status rather than psychophysiological factors is most often cited as causative in the development and predisposition of Native American youth alcoholism.

Methodological issues are frequently found within the literature such as those reported by Schaefer (1981), who reports on etiological factors including alcohol sensitivity, pleasant/unpleasant alcohol effects, and genetic factors that should be studied by culturally sensitive methodologies according to Schaefer. Oetting and Edwards (1985) report on the development of a successful Native American Youth Drug Use Survey instrument and Mail (1982) reports on studies that have made etiological conclusions and argues for an alternative methodology. Edwards and Edwards (1986) recommend a task force for identifying alcohol causative factors in specific communities, and Apostile and Miller (1975) review causative factors in order to impact future research. Leatham (1978) reviews the current status of knowledge about Native American youth alcoholism, and Estes and Heinemann (1982) review the developmental aspects of Native American youth alcoholism. Native American youths are studied at high school and college levels by Jessor (1983) who reports personality systems, perceived environment, and behavioral systems to be valid estimates of the proneness to engage in problematic behaviors including alcoholism. Finally, Andre (1979) reviews some basic causative factors.

GENDER

The literature on gender is essentially undefined from a research perspective. There is yet to accrue a sufficient amount of data to define the major issues in this area. Because of the prevalence of sex differences in other literature, it is projected as a major factor to be expected to be found in Native American youth alcoholism. However, that has yet to become extant. The few papers that do exist basically are descriptive in nature and begin to move toward the definition of the problem that is, at best, no more than 10 percent complete.

Forslund (1979) reports a similarly high percentage of alcohol abuse, self-reported by white and American Indian male and female youths. These individuals report their drinking behaviors in some detail. A significantly higher percentage of American Indian males and females have been inebriated, report having passed out more frequently, and report being "in trouble more often as a result of drinking than is reported by white youths." The percentages run above 80 percent for both groups. Boredom is often suggested as a major factor in this literature. Swanson, Bratrude, and Brown (1971) report that in a study of forty-two American Indian children, half male and half female, that boredom was given as the main reason for severe alcohol abuse, while authors report that social acceptance is the actual reason. The suggested consequences of alcohol abuse among these children include sexual promiscuity, illegitimate pregnancy, delinquency, physical complications, and suicide. Clearly, there is not yet in the literature a formulation sufficient to allow determination of which of these variables are independent, which dependent, and which are covariants. Clearly, a path analysis is needed to sort through these variables. However, Swanson et al (1971) report that respect for individual autonomy and its implied permissiveness is a significant factor in determining the quantity of alcohol consumed. This is also suggested to be related to denial of alcohol as a drug. Webster (1983) reports that 29 percent of American Indian women report boredom as the reason for alcohol consumption and abuse and report rates excess of others that they know. Some 32 percent of the women excuse themselves for their drinking, 44 percent report having guilt, and 40 percent report frequent blackouts as a result of drinking. Among children, age ten to twelve, 12 percent of females abuse alcohol, and the level of use is reported to increase with age. The significant topic here appears to be the respect for individual autonomy and its implied permissiveness toward alcohol consumption. This may have significant community implications in that it is a community standard toward permissiveness that may allow other variables to drive the alcohol consumption.

A profile of the female Native American youth alcohol abuser is beginning to merge. Hurlburt and Gade (1984) report that American Indian females are more extroverted and tough minded than white female alcoholics.

Wilmore (1979) also attempts a profile of American Indian female alcohol abusers and discusses treatment issues. Wilsnack (1980) concludes that denial of social obligations is a male role orientation that predicts alcohol abuse and dependency. Presumably, the denial of social obligations would not be a significant factor among females, although those data are not forthcoming.

In conclusion, although there are some rudimentary profile data available, both from an interpersonal and a sociological standpoint. There is yet to be issued a systematic path analysis that looks at all of the relevant factors in determining alcohol consumption. This literature has yet to reach a point where symptom is separated from cause and, indeed, most of the proposed etiological variables are more covariant than independent and dependent variables.

POLICY AND PREVENTION

Several salient themes pervade the literature on policy and prevention. These include among others risk factors, levels of prevention, treatment methodology, and the impact of policy.

The two most obvious risk factors in the literature are membership in minority groups, most particularly Native Americans, and within that risk factor, being young or of school age. These factors are treated in numerous volumes including United States Indian Health Service (1973), Drew (1981), Trimble (1982), and numerous others. Within Native American youth, sex is a significant risk factor as a larger number of males are substance abusers than are females (United States Indian Health Services, 1977; Helmick, McClure, and Mitchell, 1977; and others). The severity and type of substance abuse within school children is correlated with other risk factors among these children (Alaska Native Health Board, Risk Analysis, 1975). These higher risk factors for alcohol abuse among youth have led Drew (1981) to recommend that primary and secondary prevention should be published on this particular subgroup. Drew is not alone in this suggestion and, in fact, it pervades the prevention literature.

The presence of risk factors within the family structure is also clearly indicated. Bergman (1977) reviews the generational effects as a risk factor in the previously held belief that removal of children from alcoholic using homes would reduce the incidence of alcohol use among the young. This approach is clearly rejected. However, Steit and Nicolich (1977) point out that the absence of a father--either by death, unemployment, or neglect--constitutes significant risk factors in alcohol abuse among Native American youth. They further indicate that as the time the father spends with the child increases, the rate of consumption decreases. Interestingly, there is a correlation between abuse and fluency in the Indian language as well as living off of the reservation. All of these appear as well to be family-related risk factors. Anthropological risk factors are also indicated (Everett, 1972), and in some reports these anthropological differences are quite specific as in the suggestion or report that many Zuni alcoholics believe that they are possessed (Nelson, 1977). Genetics may also be considered a family related-risk factor. The suggestion is advanced that American Indians genetically are unprepared to drink in moderation owing to metabolism differences and alcohol sensitivity factors (Trimble, 1984). It is interesting to note that among treatment programs that claim success, there is a unifying thread of the development of social support networks. One may speculate a hypothetical linkage between success in treatment and the development of social support networks.

Prevention levels are frequently discussed and constitute major themes in the policy and prevention literature. Andre (1979) suggests the primary, secondary, and tertiary level concept in which primary prevention has as its goal education to strengthen individual and family for the purpose of resisting alcohol, where secondary intervention has as its goal the development of risk factors and prediction based upon them, and the tertiary level being oriented to treatment. Prevention typically encompasses education as for example, the development of a film on responsible alcohol consumption by beer distributors (Brewers Digest, 1979), general information on the effects of alcohol on the body (Briskin, 1980), and the suggestion that education and prevention should be specific to the type of abuse within a specifically defined ethnic group (Messolonghites, 1979). Trimble (1982) has suggested that prevention training has exhibited conflicting themes of culturally encapsulated approaches versus cultural and tribal specific orientations. This conflict has led to some potential reduction in the effectiveness of prevention training.

Irrespective of prevention training, prevention methods have been suggested to include such procedures as providing information, changing attitudes, assisting in problem solving, designing coping strategies, improving interpersonal communication and organizing support networks (Schinke, Schilling, Gilchrist, Barth, Bobo, Trimble, and Cvetkovich (1985) prevention through improvement in interpersonal skills is also commonly found (Martin, Ward, and Newman, 1982). Group therapy has been evaluated for its efficacy in dealing with Native American youth alcoholism and pan substance abuse. Schinke, Schilling, and Gilchrist (1986) report that ten weeks of hourly group intervention had moderately successful results with twelve year old Native American children. Interestingly, the involvement of peers in prevention and treatment has met with some success, particularly where peer managed self-control has implications for significant reduction in consumption as reported by Carpenter, Lyons, and Miller (1985). The theme of peer relations is also reported by White (1983) in his dissertation on treatment. He reports that the need for improvement in peer relationships, destigmatization, awareness of high risk membership, knowledge of early warning signs, awareness of social support networks, and recognition that alcoholism is a disease and not a moral issue are important features important to any prevention treatment program. This is consistent with the notion that emotional risk factors may also predispose alcohol abuse within this group, and these include anger, frustration, and boredom (United States Indian Health Service, 1973). Beauvais and La Boueff (1985) call for local community involvement in alcoholism prevention efforts in Native American communities.

Perhaps the most significant policy impact is to be found, albeit subtly, from studies on the definitions of alcoholism. It has long been suggested that the symptoms of alcoholism were derived in their definitions from the behaviors of white drinkers and, hence, created cultural bias in their application and, because of the limited cultural sample, were not universal symptoms.

In particular, the suggestion was made that behavioral symptoms are more culturally biased than physiological symptoms. However, Whitaker (1980) in a twenty year longevity study concluded that American Indian and white drinkers are more alike in that the major difference is accrued to the incidence of heavy drinking rather than to cultural factors that obscured the definitions of behavioral symptoms. Authors too numerous to cite also argue for the need of involving representation from cultural groups in the determination of policy for dealing with substance abuse within those cultural groups, and it is often suggested that the absence of such local cultural input is sufficient reason to predispose failure in any prevention treatment program or policy determination pursuant to that. Thus the state of the literature at present gives an unclear conclusion as to the necessity and the impact of the involvement of cultural representation in policy determination. While in many cases it seems clearly and strongly implicated, in other cases it may predispose untoward definitions and assumptions based more upon belief systems than data.

RESERVATIONS

The principal issues found in the existing literature on American Indian youth alcoholism in the setting of reservations divides itself into three categories. The permissiveness, antipermissiveness hypothesis on community involvement in alcohol consumption; the statistical analysis of alcohol consumption and its related factors; and cross-cultural factors in alcohol consumption.

The permissiveness hypothesis has been described in previous sections and basically deals with the idea that within the American Indian culture there is a respect for individual autonomy that implies a permissiveness toward consumption. Pemberton and Harper (1974) report that permissiveness as indicated as indicative of abuse is a significant factor in alcohol consumption. Conversely, the presence of inhibitory pressures reduces alcohol as evidenced by the Leech Lake Reservation Youth Center activities program. This is suggested as an alternative to traditional social work which does not have peer status, and thus, does not have the function of peer pressure. By implication, the anti-permissiveness hypothesis is suggested indirectly in papers such as that by Pinto (1973). This is a review of the literature on drinking and substance abuse among American Indian youth, and after reviewing the literature, the author concludes that the educational system should be turned over to Indian groups and that only those Indian groups who want alcohol and suicide prevention programs should have them. This paper is a good example of the permissiveness effect. Cockerham (1975) found a strong tolerance of and permissiveness toward cohort drinking by American Indian youth. The permissiveness is here demonstrated at the peer group level on the Wind River Indian Reservation. The presence of implied approval by peer group cohorts is indicated as a factor supporting consumption.

The number of articles on statistical analyses is growing. Buehlmann reports that between 48 and 55 percent of hospital visits on the Yankton Sioux were alcohol related or had alcohol related factors. He further indicates that 97 percent of the arrests on that reservation were also alcohol-related. Delk (1974) reports that 80 percent of the dropouts of American Indian reservation schools had alcohol arrest records. Forslund (1974) reports that although alcohol abuse is reported to vary between eighty and ninety percent on reservations, drug abuse has significantly less of an effect by percentage. As measured on the Wind River Reservation, 79.8 percent of the males and 81.1 percent of the females had tried no drugs including marijuana or others; 12.5 percent of the males and 7 percent of the females had used marijuana but no other drugs, and 6 percent of the males and 9 percent of the females had used both.

As for causative factors with statistical analysis, Weast (1972) reviews the evidence on how alcohol consumption is related to specific psychosocial factors, and reports that anomie predicts learned heavy drinking patterns in American Indian but not white youths. He finds a statistically significant difference between these two groups in which Sproles' anomie scale successfully predicts the learned heavy drinking pattern.

Cross-cultural factors run though numerous topics beyond those found in the reservation, but with specific context on reservations Topper (1980) reports a method for studying alcohol behavior at three levels: cultural, social, and individual. He combines cognitive anthropology with functional analysis to assist individuals in cultures against alcohol abuse behavior. Because of significant cultural differences with data, data on whites do not apply to American Indians. Specific results are here reported to culturally specific Navajo alcoholism factors. Tyler (1982) reports a design of culturally appropriate psychosocial services for Sioux Indian alcoholism.

Thus the principal themes to be emerging in the reservation context are a statistical analysis of etiological factors, the permissiveness and anti-permissiveness argument, and the cross-cultural differences.

SOCIOLOGICAL FACTORS:
CULTURAL TRANSITION DEMOGRAPHICS AND
SOCIOECONOMIC DEPRIVATIONS

The literature is this chapter is by far the most
difficult and challenging to organize into central and
relevant themes, principally because of the conflict
between external and internal influences. The
external influences of traditional sociological study
define specific areas of interest to the field of
sociology, including demographic data of a
comparative, specific, regional, and general nature.
However, there are specific internal factors of
emerging interest to the area of Native American
youth alcoholism that are relatively more unique to
that field, and less well-defined within
traditional sociological study. For example, the areas
of the development of alcohol consumption behavior
among Native American youth is critical to this
field of inquiry, though not well-defined within
traditional sociology. Similarly, the area of
administration and management of Native American
schools is made problematic by the presence of alcohol
consumption. This appears to be a relatively unique
area having little literary definition in
traditional sociology. The internal and external
conflicting factors find some areas of mutual
concurrence in the literature on rates of consumption
and culturally based rates of consumption. Given
this preamble, the following eight areas or major
themes were identified within the sociological
factors literature on Native American youth
alcoholism: general demographics, specific demographics, regional demographics, comparative demographics, alcohol consumption, general culturally based
rates, and schools.

General Demographics

Adams (1975) studies social demographics and reports
citations on a full range of reviewed articles having
implications for Native Americans in general, but
also includes Native American alcoholism. Andre
(1979) reports on a study of Native American alcohol
patterns with a focus on historical patterns,
recent cultural changes, and Native American specific
patterns as well as firewater myths. Explanations
for these results include (1) poor role models, (2)
effects of Indian wars, (3) reservation confinement,
(4) early alcohol exposure, and (5) lack of
cultural assimilation with alcohol experiences and
others. Andre follows up in 1980 with a study on
the impact of alcohol on morbidity and morality and
found that 70 percent of Indian health services are

delivered to Indians with alcohol and alcohol-related problems. The topic of services as it impacts general demographics is also found in other literature.

For example, Baine and Goodluck (1984) report on a federally funded project for the development and dissemination of information on Native American youth services including substance abuse. Attneave (1982) reports on a description of general demographic characteristics of Native American and Alaskan Natives, including the fetal alcohol syndrome and the relationships of alcohol to suicide. Heath (1983) surveyed beliefs and behaviors about Native American alcohol use, and relates initiation and continuation of alcohol consumption behavior to cultural factors. Heath also sought to dispel the firewater myth as have numerous other authors. McBride (1980) reviews the epidemiological data on Native American youth alcoholism and reports on it in an extensive review. Mueller (1986) surveys children's books depicting Native Americans and found more realistic themes including alcohol topics in the recent decade. Noble (1978) reports on an extensive review and synthesis of the alcohol literature from a general demographics approach. Although this article covers numerous ethnic groups, Native American youth are specifically included. Topper (1981) reports on an analysis of methodological differences in the study of cultural drinking patterns within the general demographics literature. The basic thesis is that different methods will result in different conclusions on general demographics. In the United States Indian Health Service Division, Resource Coordination Office of Program Statistics Report for 1978, there is contained natality and mortality rates for Native Americans by geographical area. This has considerable significance, given the high rate of natality and mortality as a result of alcohol consumption. The National Institute on Alcohol Abuse and Alcoholism in its final report in 1975 dealing with general demographics gives the results of a random sample of 1974 high school students who were given questionnaires concerning their adolescent alcohol drinking behavior. These data revealed a relationship between adolescent drinking behavior and a full array of general demographic factors. Vizenor (1982) estimates that 50 percent of Native American tribal populations are chemically dependent, while 40 percent are affected. He also reports tribal drinking is different from non-tribal drinking, and that tribal inhibition is effective in the control of drinking.

Specific Demographics

The literature on specific demographics deviates from the general demographics literature in that it deals with specific tribes and the cultural differences unique to those groups. For example, Allison (1974) reports on a thorough and in-depth study on education factors of the Mesquakie who have not responded positively to mainstreaming and who have experienced most of the historically negative effects of Native American education. Alcoholism is among the list of the most negative aspects in the Mesquakie.

Broudy and May (1983) report that Navajo mortality and natality rates are linked to modernization factors including alcoholism. Ferguson (1976), also studying Navajos, reports Navajo specific drinking patterns that are different from other tribal groups. Simeone (1981) describes the takeover cycle of the Upper Tanana and Upper Copper River regions of the eastern interior of Alaska. In this takeover cycle, one member drinks for several days to several weeks, and then passes on the drinking to another member so that drinking is perpetuated. Stevens, in a study of the Passamaquoddy, discusses the inclusion of alcohol in their cultural patterns. Stratton (1981) argues that unfavorable socioeconomic conditions were found to impact the rates of alcohol among Oklahoma Native American tribes. Topper (1974) in the study of Navajo drinking patterns and long-term economic development found that there is a relationship to problem drinking in economic underdevelopment. Youth drinking is attributed, in part, to a culturalization stress.

Regional Demographics

Regional demographics has to do with the demographics that occur within geographical regions and may cross over the specific demographics of tribes or subcultures. For example, Adams (1971) reports on the Michigan Interim Action Committee on Indian Problems in which the state recommendations for Native American education, health, employment, and its Commission on Indian Affairs is reported. Recommendations include remedial action for alcoholism. Alu Like Inc. (1979) studies the native Hawaiian population to determine mental health service needs. They found the highest needs in alcohol, family violence, and adolescent suicide and drug abuse. These data have implications for involving the extant and functioning extended family in treatment. The most extensive regional demographic literature is that in the series of reports by Attneave and Beiser (1982) on Service Networks and

Patterns of Utilization: Mental Health   Programs, Indian Health Service,   Volumes 1,   3,   4,   5,   and 9. Regional demographics,   service, and administrative reports are   included.   A   history of the development and operation of each of the   eight Indian   Health Service Mental Health area offices   is   included. Recommendations   on continuing problems such as alcohol and   drug abuse   are   included.   An overview and introduction are given   in Volume 1, while Volume 3 discusses Alaska Area Office development of   specific mental health programs such as alcohol   and   others. Volume   4   deals with Albuquerque and its population and culture, including Pueblo,   Ute,   Jicarilla Apache, and Mescalero Apache.   These   are   described   in terms   of   service   needs   including alcoholism. Volume   5 deals with the Billings Regional   Office, and Volume 9 with the Portland Area Office.   This   last volume   includes   information   on   alcohol   abuse, treatment,   and planning in that regional area. Clearly, the demographics differ by region.

Longie   (1984) found significantly greater alcohol consumption in childhood among rural rather than urban Native American   regions.   Negrette   (1982)   reports that United   States Native   Americans exhibit   more opiate   and   methadone use   than   Canadian   Native Americans.

Comparative Demographics

The   final   area   of   demographics has   to   do   with comparative   demographics   in   which   specific comparisons   are   made   between ethnic   groups or tribal cultures.   These can cross regional and tribal specific fields.   For example,   the Canadian Journal of Public Health (1982) reports that Canadian Native Americans   are identified as high risk for alcoholism, motivated by a desire to escape the harshness of their life-styles,   and this differs from other   groups   in the same region.   Cohen (1982)   reports   that Native American   alcoholism is two to four   times   the national level,   and greater than any other minority group with respect to severity of the presenting problem.   Second, he reports that five of   the   first ten causes of Native American deaths   are alcohol-related   and   that   drinking   patterns   are   not monolithic,   though some specificity does exist.   He further argues that the etiology includes   (1)   few sanctions on   youth   drinking,   (2)   high frequency alcohol   role   models,   and   (3)   multi-generational factors are involved in which the role modeling effect passes the alcoholism   down from parent to child. Cockerham (1976) reports that Native American youths are more likely than white youths   to   try   alcohol. He reports no differences in Native Americans and

whites in rate of consumption once the behavior
has begun. Gregory (1975) compared black Native
American and white alcohol abuse rates in Oklahoma
with Native Americans and found that Native American
males are the highest in consumption rates; black males
are greater than females, who are lowest in
juvenile delinquency arrest rates, but second
highest in the adult population, and third, that
69 percent of treated alcoholics were Native
Americans, 18 percent were black, and 19 percent were
white. Everette (1976) reports on the NIMH Conference
on Anthropology and Alcoholism. He reports that
methodological approaches to the observation of
drinking behavior can impact the results of studies.
He also finds cross-cultural perspectives in this
literature and multidisciplinary approaches. Jilek
(1973) found Native American homicide to be alcohol-
related in Canadian Native Americans, particularly
Coast Salish. He describes the development of anomic
depression from alcohol use in this particular
group. In a subsequent paper (1975), he presents
the cultural conflict factors in the Coast Salish
Indian alcoholism and differentiates it from other
groups. Locklear (1985) reports on a cross-cultural
study of the definition of mental health as commonly
used by Native American blacks and whites. Although
common themes were found, the emphasis given to
each varies across groups. Native Americans had the
highest tolerance for alcohol and violence behavior.

Alcohol Consumption

Age, income, and sex were found to affect the mental
health definition differentially. Oetting (1980)
compared Native American and non-Native American
youths for poly-drug use at grades seven through
twelve. He found that Native Americans had greater
alcohol and poly-drug consumption and argued for
the necessity for culturally sensitive intervention strategies. Olsen (1982) studied the self-
reports of adolescents, indicating 84 percent of Native
American high school students have experimented with
alcohol while 43 percent regularly consume. Their
rates were found to be similar to non-Native
Americans. Poulson, Pettibone, and Willey (1978)
studied alcohol self-reports related to Anglo,
Hispanic, and Native American problem drinking to
several psychological and demographic variables.
He found that ethnicity is not a significant
predictor, but that effective predictors include peer
factors, veteran status, and social alienation. Rachal
(1971) reported on an extensive survey of 13,000
secondary education students drawn from a nationwide
probability sample and used to assess alcohol behavior

cross cultures.   Segal (1983) gives us an overview of the cross-cultural alcohol literature on Alaskan Native Americans and Senay (1983) argues for group specificity and treatment needs including   Native American alcoholism.   Wanberg (1978) compares demographics on seventy Native Americans,   forty-seven   blacks, seventy-seven Hispanics,   and seventy-four white alcoholics.   All groups   reported   social and vocational   disruption   with   Native American disruption   greater than all other   groups.   No differences in reasons were found among groups. Wingert   and Fifield   (1985)   report   on   cross cultural   characteristics in inhalant use among Native American boarding school students as compared to nonusers. Similarities to the mainstream cultural groups were noted.

General and Culturally Based Rates

The   literature on rates,   including general and culturally based rates, is somewhat similar in demographics but sufficiently different to warrant their being considered as a separate category or theme.   Basically, the rate literature has to do with the consumption patterns and the percentage of the population initiating and continuing and abusing alcohol.   This may be a general factor for all Native Americans, or it may be for specific subcultures in tribes.   The general hypothesis is that the rate of consumption is greater among Native Americans   than others, although there are some specific variations on this argument in which the age of initiation and the possibility of continuation   are   argued. Barnes (1986) on cultural   rate specificity, finds cultural differences in demographics in a study of adolescent alcohol consumption,   prevalence, and patterns among secondary students.   Native Americans and Anglos had the highest consumption rate among six ethnic groups studied in this rate-based cultural comparison.   Other rate-based cultural comparisons are found in Gregory's 1975 work in which black, Native American, and white alcohol consumption patterns in Oklahoma are reported with Native Americans suggested to be the highest consumers.
       Goldstein and Oetting (1979) report on a survey of poly-drug use in 276 Native American secondary education students and found significantly higher rates among Native Americans than among non-Native American college students.   Oetting (1977) also reports on culturally based rate data in a sample of 3,000 Native American alcoholic adolescents with respect to their poly-drug use.   The rate was found to be two to three times the nonculturally based rate.   Factors cited include peer influence,

broken homes, social isolation, and despair about the future.

The literature that is not culturally specific with regard to rate has to do with the general rate factors in comparing all Native Americans to other ethnic groups. The principal theme of this literature is that the rate of consumption is higher among Native Americans than non-Native Americans. For example, Green (1981) reports on surveys conducted between 1972 and 1975 showing a child Native American alcohol use rate increase from 59 percent to 90 percent. This differs from some estimates which show a 50 percent use rate. The low socioeconomic status and the high consumption rate factor was again found as implied causative relationship. Hammerschlag (1982) reports that the Native American alcoholism rate is 50 to 90 percent. Kraus and Buffler (1979) report that alcoholism is significantly higher in Aleut, Athabascan, Yupik, Inupiat, Tlingit, Haida, and Tsimpshian than other Alaskan non-Native American groups. However in contravention of this generally held hypothesis, there is a report by the Idaho State Journal of 1982 that argues that data are grossly in error because they do not define (1) individual drinking (2) tribal drinking, and (3) Indian drinking, in concluding on these general rate differences. They argue for understanding from a multi-factor analysis approach in that the rate data are thus tainted. The two final themes, having the greatest specificity for Native American youth alcoholism, and being unique to this literature and relatively undifferentiated by the traditional sociological methods literature, are the themes on developmental and school failure in alcohol consumption.

Liban and Smart (1982) demonstrate the peer effect in the development of drinking behavior among Native American youths. They used a matched sample procedure that controlled for excessive extraneous variation and indeed, concluded that one of the major factors in the development of alcohol consumption among Native American youth is peer drinking and its transmission by that vehicle. Longie (1984) found significantly greater alcohol use among Native American children in urban than rural areas, and that the development rate was greater in an urban population than a non-urban population. May (1982) reviewed the alcohol prevalence literature among Native Americans and found that the consumption development rate was greater among Native American youth.

In a subsequent 1982 paper, May studied developmental aspects of Native American youth alcohol behavior and found that high consumption patterns were common to adolescent Native Americans, but that drug, nonalcohol substances consumption was a transitory phenomena in this group. Alcohol consumption behavior at high levels is more likely to develop in the absence of cultural identity among Native Americans. This finding is irrespective of whether the Native American individual identified with Native American culture or mainstream culture and argues that the absence of acculturation in either group is a major factor in the development of alcohol consumption. The suggestion is made that alcohol consumption behavior develops in the absence of a perceived support system. Oetting (1983) presents a typology for Native American drug use. Eight types are presented and based upon individual social and personal characteristics. In a previous 1982 paper, Oetting reports on a study of 9,000 Native American children in three grade clusters, examining their poly-drug developmental use and patterns of consumption. Native Americans in grades seven through twelve had higher exposure to all drugs. Inhalants were more commonly tried among Native Americans than non-Native American youths. Native Americans start marijuana inhalant use at a younger age, but this is a transitory phenomena. Finally, Native American culture provides some protection against some serious drug use. Subsequently, in 1982, Oetting reports a summary of Native American youth drug use literature further documenting the crisis of consumption levels in this group. He cites prejudice, poverty, and political wardship as continuing factors in this paper which was co-authored with Beauvias, entitled "Drug Use Among Native American Youths: Summary and Findings, 1975-1981." Again, Oetting (1979) reported a study of poly-drug use and development among Native American adolescents and cites such factors as cultural heritage and acculturation, multilife problems and poverty as significant factors in developmental use. Intragroup versus nonuser comparisons were also made by Oetting in this paper. The series had begun in collaboration with Goldstein in 1979 and again in 1979 with Goldstein in "Native American Drug Use". Oetting reports a sample of 3,000 Native American adolescent poly-drug users in which the rate was found to be two to three times the norm, based principally upon peer influence and broken homes, social isolation, and despair about the future. Royce (1981) distinguishes the difference in drinking behavior from alcoholism and differentiating adolescents from adult alcohol problems. Native Americans are included in this study. Finally, Stanchfield (1979) gives a report that includes research indicating emotional and stimulus generalization factors in alcohol mythologies. The developmental aspects of Native American drinking acquisition are included in studies related to the myth. Watts and Lewis (1988) argue for local community involvement, and for a focus by the federal government on mediating structures (family, etc.) as well as traditional approaches.

This is augmented by two other papers. Walker (1976) studied the effects of parental drinking on adolescent drinking behavior by surveying forty-four Native American adolescents. Introduction age for females was thirteen and for males it was fourteen, with beer being preferred. Consumption increased with age. Weibel-Orlando (1984) studied Native American youth alcohol patterns and found factors contributing to use that included (1) parental tolerance, (2) belief in individual autonomy, (3) cultural acceptance of altered states of consciousness, and (4) beer preference. The major factors in the development of alcohol consumption behaviors, on balance, appear to be the age of initiation, the means of initiation and maintenance--principally, peer pressure and parental role modeling, and altered states of consciousness and the secondary gains from those.

Schools

The literature on schools as it impacts Native American alcohol consumption among youth is found early on in the literature on rate comparisons in which Native American youths are shown to be higher in consumption than other non-Native American groups. For example, the Goldstein and Oetting paper of 1979, surveying poly-drug use in 276 Native American post-secondary education students indicating a significantly higher rate, is typical of this literature. Holmgren, Fitzgerald, and Carmen (1983) relate student drinking patterns to alienation that was found to be higher among Native American youths. The suggestion being that at the school age, child alienation is a significant factor in drinking. Horton and Annolora (1974) report the major cause of dropouts from Native American schools is alcohol use. Klinekole (1979) studied problems of Native American youth in boarding schools and found that alcohol was the major problem in school management. This suggests problems in administration, and Forslund (1978) administered questionnaires to ninth-grade through twelfth-grade Native American and white alcohol consumers and concluded in opposition to the hypothesis that cultural differences exist. They find no significant differences in personal effect and positive social factors between Native American and white secondary education students in Fremont County, Wyoming. However, Miller, Helmic, and McClure (1978) studied the magnitude of Native American student drinking problems at Mt. Edgecumbe Boarding School. Maximum estimate of alcohol abuse was 29 percent. Consistently, the literature suggests that alcohol use among Native American students is problematic in the administration of schools.

In conclusion, this literature on sociological factors is different from the other literature in that while it does not lack research definition, it does lack organization. This organizational conflict appears to arise from external versus internal factors of influence in the developing of the literature. Factors specific to Native American youth are often at odds with methodology found in sociological literature per se, while the sociological literature is often lacking in direct relevance to the Native American populations. It may even be that a specific ethnographic method with Native Americans is necessary for the study of alcohol consumption and development problems. While traditional sociological methods may be more appropriate to administration and demographic issues, they can, by their very presence, obscure and alter results when being applied to a specific Native American group. Basically, the Heisenburg principal appears to apply here.

SUICIDE

The main topic to be found in suicide is the rate versus type data, and the role of alcohol in the act itself. Berman (1979) reports on suicide among the rural sample of Shoshone and Paiute Native Americans. The rate is reported to be related to alcoholism directly in 86 percent of completed suicides. These suicides are described as alcohol-related, unplanned, and impulsive acts. Blackwood (1978) studied the role of alcohol and suicide mortality and morbidity in Alaska while Fox, Manitowabi, and Ward (1984) found a significant decrease in suicide attempts among Manitoulin Native Americans by (1) including family members in alcohol group treatment, (2) producing a nonalcoholic community feast, (3) enabling youth to gain stature through community services, and (4) school-based alcohol counselors who promoted self-esteem, traditional values, and alcohol education. The type/rate arguments are brought forth by Grove, Linge, and Linge (1979) among others. These authors report on Eskimo suicide rates, which have quadrupled to a level of two per thousand of completed suicides, while attempted suicides were at a rate of ten per thousand of the adult population. However, the attempts were principally among youth. Miller (1979) reports that the typical Native American suicide profile of Southwestern people is a young, unmarried male with an unskilled job. These are among completed suicides. Shore (1972) reports on suicide rates among American Indians of the Pacific Northwest and finds a rate of completed suicide at 2.8 per thousand, with a ratio of sixteen attempts per committed suicide. A typical profile is a thirty-year-old male, single or separated, who hangs or shoots himself. The typical attempter, however, was the young Native American female ingesting drugs who had recently had a quarrel with a family member where the attempt was put forth for the purpose of controlling relationships or expressing anger at home. Significantly, these attempts were associated with alcohol. Spaulding (1985-86) reports on Ojibwa suicide rates and suggests that the completion rate is 6.17 per thousand. The typical completed suicide profile is that of a young male who uses a firearm in an alcohol related act. This profile was found in 50 percent of the cases.

TREATMENT

The essential literature issues on treatment of Native American youth alcoholics include methodology, cultural differences, and program reviews. One of the principal features in the methodological issue on treatment involves the argument of specificity versus generality in treatment methodology. For example, Bain and Taylor (1979) assessed counseling skills relevant to alcohol abusers and sought to identify specific and unique therapeutic needs about alcohol abusers. They pursued an answer to the question to what extent counselors need therapeutic skills that are specific to these identified needs. In this study, Native American youth alcohol abusers were included. Baird (1978) found an inverse correlation between certain specific attributes of therapists and the outcome of their treatment. For example, authoritarianism and social restriction were found to be inversely correlated with the extent of academic training among Alaskan alcohol treatment professionals. This trait is suggested by Berg as desirable in a personnel selection factor. Westermeyer and Neider (1984) found treatment outcomes in Native American alcohol abusers to be significantly enhanced where there was (1) less parental loss, (2) no prior marriages, (3) compliance, and (4) having Native American friends. In a very interesting study on other correlates, Hudson (1981) found that agoraphobia was a significant factor in successful treatment. In his 1981 paper, he reports that social phobias, in particular agoraphobia, are prevalent among Native American alcoholics and suggests that treatment should be directed to this possible causative factor. The types of treatment intervention have also been studied. Merrill (1974) reports on an in-depth study of the efficacy of group psychotherapy with adolescents in Native American boarding schools. He found a decrease in depression, anxiety, physical problems, and anger as well as increases in self-understanding, self-concept, self-expression, verbal behavior, and successful behavior in school.

As something of an aside to the typical themes seen in the drug intervention literature, there is the Grinspoon and Bakalar (1981) report that lysergic acid diethylamide (LSD) produces powerful, short-delay effects on alcoholics that support sobriety in 50 percent of severe alcoholics. However, treatment efficacy is in dispute even by the authors. There is a significant concern about using one substance to control the abuse of another substance. However, other authors have commented on multiple substance abuse as for example, Bloome, Futterman, and Pascorosa

(1977) in which they review literature on common models, that of alcohol and opiate dependency suggesting a possible existence of a common mode of treatment. This paper also obviously diverges from the specificity of theme and argues for more generality in methodological treatment approaches.

The specificity argument has also been applied to specific tribes with the suggestion that these small, relatively homogeneous groups have unique requirements that must be recognized in therapy in order for the therapy to be effective. For example, Hodgson (1982) reports on a program in which Ojibwa Native Americans were trained as alcohol counselors for other drinking Ojibwas. Only former and sober alcoholics were employed as counselors in this program and the effectiveness was argued in a positive vein.

Katz (1981) reports on alcohol therapists with Cree and Saulteaux-Ojibwa therapists and suggests that they must learn the Native American value system, develop new communication skills, and reexamine standard practices in order to be effective with Native American groups. Merker (1981) reviews problems in alcohol counseling among Omaha, Winnebago, and Sioux. Group counseling techniques specific to these groups are discussed and suggested for other practitioners. Orford (1984) approaches specificity with regard to the family and reviews the studies on alcohol treatment within the family. He provides some theoretical and family systems perspective for this approach. In a similar vein, Waite and Leudwig (1983) reviewed treatments oriented to children of alcoholics. In contravention to the ethnospecificity argument, Query (1985) found no significant etiological differences between Anglo and Native American youth alcoholics, although the Native American youth were overrepresented in the sample. Although the principal hypothesis of this literature review is far from conclusive, it is clear that the weight of evidence is in favor of specificity argument on an ethnocentric basis.

The literature on program review is important both from the standpoint of identifying attitudes of service deliverers about their own programs, but also attitudes about the community toward the program and about the recipients regarding the efficacy of the program. These program reviews are oriented along administrative issues as well as efficacy issues. Burns (1981) surveyed attitudes of Phoenix, Arizona, health professionals toward Native American alcoholics. These professionals felt more positive about the programs and services they were delivering than about their clients. There is implication here for efficacy of empathy in a successful treatment

program.   Hedin (1981) reviews   Native   American
alcohol   treatment   programs   in Albuquerque,   New
Mexico,   and finds an interrelationship between alcohol
abuse and other Native American community characteristics.   There is a coimplication of   interaction
between the community and successfulness of a program.

Kunitz (1981) reviews political, ideological
characteristics   of Native   American   alcohol
programs   and   suggests   that   these characteristics
inhibit   the   utilization of   research   findings
emanating from such programs.

Nighswander (1984)   found   among   Native   American
Aleuts and Eskimos a high   utilization   of ambulatory
care that had a significant implication for mortality
rates owing   to   alcohol-related events.   The interaction with the service agency is also reported, by
Rhodes, Marshall, and Attneave (1975) who compare the
numbers and rates of visits to Indian Health Service
offices per diagnostic code including alcoholism.

Sanders   (1985)   reviewed   the   issues,   and
recommended   that pediatricians   be trained in alcohol
interview   and   counseling skills   as   this was a
critical point   of intervention.   Shore (1984) reviews
alcohol treatment for Native American   alcoholics among
other   topics   in   a   program   review   study.
Financial considerations   were obviously of no concern
in research   program review.   For example, Dominick
(1976) reviews briefly the non-pay services for several
groups including Native Americans and youth.   Ferguson,
similarly, in 1981 reviews programs funded specifically
for   treatment of Native American alcoholism versus all
programs having   Native   Americans included in   its
treatment.   Although program   review is   clearly
present as a major theme in the   issue of treatment,
the approach and popularity of program review   and
program   evaluation   do not appear to have reached the
peak   of interest found in the previous decade.   There
appears to be less interest in program reviews than in
previous years,   at least   in this   particular   segment
of the literature.   It seems that   the existence   of
the programs has become more important   than   the
review of their efficacy.

Finally,   there   is the   issue of cultural
differences   in   Native American youth alcoholism.
This is a very popular and pervasive topic in the
literature. For example, Callahan (1981) conducted an
ethnographic needs assessment of Papago alcohol abusers
and found   (1)   no significant difference in   socioeconomic   status between   drinkers   and   nondrinkers,
(2) drinking styles to include   acute public drunk,
periodic   alcohol   abuser,   the consistent alcohol
abuser, and the alcoholic, and   (3)   the   lack of
Papago response to available intervention programs due
to   these   treatments   being   Anglo   oriented.   There

is a strong argument for the need of culturally sensitive treatment styles. This argument is further advanced by Collido (1981), who reviews the historical use of alcohol by Native Americans and presents a theoretical framework for a traditional Native American treatment program. He proposes a new theoretical approach to Native American alcoholism that recognizes cultural differences. This approach is local invasion research. Similarly, Curran (1982) describes an alcohol treatment program for Maine Indians delivered by a group called the West German Clinic. The core program was specifically designed to meet cultural needs of that group and has as one of its main arguments its cultural sensitivity from a culturally different group.

D'Arcy and Fritz (1982) studied culture differences between Saskatchewan and non-Native American's in terms of the prevalence of mental health disorders, rates of treatment, and inpatient versus outpatient percentages. They found diagnostic differences more common in private than in public agencies, and a higher frequency of mental retardation diagnoses most frequent and alcoholism diagnoses least frequent. The differences in the diagnostic frequencies are suggested to be culturally biased.

Hurlburt, Gade, and Fuqua (1982) report that Native American alcoholics had higher psychoticism in life scores and lower extroversion scores on the Eysenick Personality Questionnaire than did non-Native American alcoholics. Smith-Peterson (1983) focused on cultural differences in alcoholism among several cultures including Native Americans and furthered the argument on the efficacy in cultural differences in this treatment group. Although the preponderance of published articles favor the cultural difference argument, there is the significant paper of Flores (1983) who reports higher alcohol incidence and lower recovery rates among Native Americans and suggests the need for therapy programs that fit specific cultural values. He found that significant differences in Native American and non-Native American values, and found alcohol overrides cultural influences. Thus, Native American alcoholics are suggested to be more similar to other alcoholics than to nonalcoholic peers.

In conclusion, two main points appear to have achieved the status of consensus: (1) that method of treatment delivery must be culturally sensitive even among cultural subgroups, and (2) that treatment programs are more important by their existence than by their efficacy as indicated by program review and program evaluation. On balance, the treatment literature appears to be well-defined by the numbers and qualities of publications in this area.

URBAN VS. RURAL

The urban versus rural literature divides itself obviously into urban and rural issues and the contrast between the two.

The Alameda County, California Task Force on Youth and Alcohol Report (1980) delivered a survey of student alcohol use in Alameda County. It found (1) 16 percent of adolescents used alcohol 50 times, (2) 2 percent acknowledged drinking problems, (3) beer was most popular, (4) 62 percent of ninth graders drank beer in the last year, (5) 10 percent reported getting really drunk, (6) more alcohol was consumed by males than females, and (7) Native Americans and Anglos were ranked number one and two in consumption levels on all of the groups seen. Bittker (1973) reports that Southwest Native Americans leaving reservations acquire an ambiguous status upon entering urban life. The local agencies consider them wards of the federal government while the federal government agencies consider them beyond the reservations. Thus there is a void in services such as alcoholism prevention and treatment owing to a lack of perceived responsibility upon the transition from rural to urban. Brelsford (1977) studied rural Athabascan alcohol use including (1) systemic patterns, (2) implicit rules, (3) alcohol values, (4) the role of youth, and (5) the effects of alcohol. He recognizes the cultural factor in drinking in a rural community as significant to the problem. Cockerham (1977) studied the alcohol and poly-drug use among rural Native American and Anglo adolescents. Although both groups approve of drinking, Native American consumption is higher, and the pattern emerges in which Native Americans consume greater amounts of alcohol and marijuana whereas Anglos consume greater amounts of alcohol and hard drugs. Hill (1980) studied urban Winnebago and Santee Dakota drinking patterns and found culturally specific subculture drinking differences arguing for specificity over generality in treatment programs. Winfree (1978) studied Native American and Anglo drug use in a rural area and found differences in informal versus formal control mechanisms. Finally, Waddell (1976) studied the impact of the Arizona Intoxification Code on traditional drinking among Papago Native Americans. The law provides for detoxification and counseling centers instead of arrests as an alternative.

The urban literature includes the Jackson, Carlisi, Greenway, and Zalesnick (1981) paper that reports a study of cultural differences in the age of first experimentation in urban settings. They found Native Americans to be the earliest

experimenters   of the ethnic groups studied   in   urban
settings   in Detroit,   Baltimore,   Cincinnati,   and
Providence.   Miller   and Wittstock   (1981) surveyed
Native American alcohol consumption in St. Paul,
Minnesota. Similarly, Phillips and Phin (1981) studied
alcohol   use   and abuse   in three urban areas of
greatest   Native American concentration and recognized
specific cultural treatment requirements among the
groups studied.

Turner   (1981)   reports   that in Seattle   (1)
Native   American alcohol   dependency   is   equal to
Anglo   dependency,   (2)   the psychological   dependency on alcohol among Native Americans is   four   times
greater   than   Anglo psychological dependency, (3) 90
percent   of   Native American arrests and   32   percent
of Native   American   deaths   are alcohol-related,   and
(4)   binge drinking is a more common pattern among
Native Americans.   Walker (1981) reports on a
successful social model for alcohol treatment among
Seattle's Native Americans and argues for   specificity
in alcohol   treatment   at   the   subcultural   level.
Wieble   (1982) describes urbanization of Native
American drinking and suggests a coping strategy.
Wieble follows this with a 1979 paper in   which he
studied   four   urban   Native   American   alcohol
consumption patterns,   including   (1)   the fifth
Sunday,   (2)   Saturday   night powwow,   (3)   ritualized
weekend powwows, and   (4)   urban   Native American bars.
He found that Native Americans shift   consumption
patterns   across   situational   contacts, which   in
turn   promotes   increased consumption in specific
context.

The articles comparing and contrasting urban
versus rural   Native American consumption patterns
include the 1982 Wieble paper that reports   on   Native
American   alcohol   consumptions   in   urban
environments   as   a coping strategy.   There is a
review   of   the cultural context differences in rural
versus urban differences in these patterns.   Weibel-
Orlando, Weisner, and Long (1984) compared rural versus
urban California Native American alcohol consumption
and   found   (1)   that fear was greater among males than
females,   (2)   urban consumption increased from
adolescence to young adult at   a higher consumption
level in urban than in   rural   settings,   (3)   urban
consumption is greater than rural   consumption,   and
(4) they   recommend   involvement of the family   in
support group   counseling   or   remediation   both   in
rural   and   urban communities.   The   United States
American Indian   Policy Review Commission   in   1976
studied rural versus   urban   non-reservation needs   and
found (1) a review of administrative   procedures   for
services,   (2)   projected needs, and   (3)   explored
alternatives in alcoholism as well as other needs

areas.   Finally,   Hahn (1982) compares   alcohol   and marijuana   use between   rural   and   urban secondary students.   He found   that urban use was greater than rural   use   among Native American students.   Neale Query   (1985) reports   that   drug   abuse among non-rural   North   Dakota   Native American   youth   was significantly   more   likely   to   lead   to involvement in   state treatment programs than drug   abuse   in   a comparable   group of rural youth.   No significant differences   in these groups were found between white and Native American   youth, although   the   Native American, as   with   other   literature   and substances, were found to be over represented.

NATIVE AMERICAN YOUTH
AND ALCOHOL

1

ACCIDENTAL DEATH

American Automobile Association, 2nd National DWI Conference Proceedings. Held in Rochester, MN: 40 May - 1 June 1979. 188 p Falls Church, Va., 1979. 188p.

The Second National DWI Conference focused on the theme of "DWI counter-attack tie-ins to identification and treatment of problem drivers." The primary goal of the multidisciplinary conference was to strengthen the ties between DWI programs and community agencies working to help people with alcohol problems. Among the subjects addressed are the uses of identification and assessment scales for problem drinkers, and treatment program considerations for special population groups. Findings from studies on the DWI population and treatment system are offered. Finally, alcoholism diagnostic and treatment efforts conducted at the Mayo Clinic in Rochester, Minnesota are described. Native Americans are discussed in this volume.

Hursh, C. Yukon, Impaired Driver Study: Phase 2. Ottawa, Ontario, Canada: Department of Indian and Northern Affairs, 1981, 105 p.

The purpose of this study was to: (1) supplement existing information about Yukon impaired drivers, and Yukon policies and procedures regarding impaired drivers; and (2) to identify countermeasures used elsewhere that could be applied to Yukon offenders. A summary of the Phase 1 study is provided, and a copy of the Yukon Impaired Drivers' Program Evaluation Form is appended. 23 Ref.

Nusbaumer, M. R., and Zusman, M. E. "Autos, Alcohol, and Adolescence: Forgotten Concerns and Overlooked Linkages," Journal of Drug Education, 11 (2): 167-178, 1981.

An attempt was made to locate and better understand a group of adolescents who ride with a drinking driver but do not drink and drive themselves. This group was compared to those who both drink and drive and ride with a drinking driver, and those who do neither. Specific attention was given to selected sociodemographic characteristics and alcohol-related attitudes and behaviors as group discriminating factors. It is suggested that the practice of riding with a drinking driver may be causally linked to the eventual practice of drinking and driving.

2

BIOMEDICAL FACTORS

Aase, J.M. "Fetal Alcohol Syndrome in American Indians: A High Risk Group," Neurobehavioral Toxicology and Teratology, 3(2):153-156

A number of factors which might increase the risk for fetal alcohol syndrome (FAS) in Native American groups are examined. Cultural influences, fertility, patterns of alcohol consumption and abuse, and perhaps dietary and metabolic differences may be involved. The suspicion of increased occurrence of FAS in the Indian population is presently based upon incomplete or anecdotal evidence, but it is noted that studies are now underway to define actual prevalence rates in some of these groups. 12 Ref.

Asse, Jon. U. "Hair zinc levels in children with fetal alcohol syndrome and their mothers," Research in Progress. Rockville, Md.: Indian Health Service, date unknown.

This study is focused upon determining whether zinc deficiency is associated with fetal alcoholic syndrome (FAS) in the offspring of alcoholic Indian women. The authors research design includes utilization of two groups of subjects: The first, consisting of Indian women (Navajo) who drink at least 3 oz. of alcohol or more per day for extended periods during pregnancy and the second, consisting of children clinically diagnosed with FAS and their mothers. Using a matching process the author then plans to collect samples of scalp hair, serum and urine (from both mother and infant). Comparisons will then be made to correlate findings between alcoholic and control females and their offspring with the incidence of FAS. LAT

Baxter, J.D.; Julien, G.; Tewfik, T.L.; Ilecki, H.J.; Crago, M.B., "Observations on the Prevalence of Ear

Disease in the Inuit and Cree Indian School Population of Kuujjuaraapik," Journal of Otolaryngol. 1986, Feb. 15 (1). p. 25-30.

In the last twenty years it has been recognized that hearing loss as the result of middle ear infection and/or noise exposure is a major problem among Canadian Inuit. In the past ten years in the Eastern Canadian Arctic attempts have been made to alleviate the problem and physicians, audiologists and educators have been involved in treatment, training programs and research with varying degrees of success. In the last few years the Quebec Inuit have become more aware of these problems and have asked for assistance. Whatever evolves, Inuit cooperation and advice is essential; their cultural identity must be respected if any project is to be successful. In February, 1984, a program outline working paper entitled "Program Quebec" was circulated by Project Nord-Laval University. The goal of the program was "to ensure the integrity of hearing for the Inuit by preventing hearing loss, identifying hearing loss, and minimizing the effects of hearing loss." In October, 1985, a Pilot Project involving the school population at Kuujjuaraapik was carried out involving personnel from the Project Nord-Laval University, the Department of Otolaryngology and the School of Human Communication Disorders-McGill University.

California Urban Indian Health Council, Fetal Alcohol Syndrome Prevention Program: Inservice Training Curriculum. Oakland, CA., 1981, 11p.

The purpose of this training seminar is to provide the clinician and staff of Indian health programs with the knowledge to educate patients about the fetal alcohol syndrome, identify Indian women of child-bearing age whose drinking appears to create a risk for the unborn, and to set up their own referral systems for assigning high risk patients to appropriate services.

Counts, G.W.; Gregory, D.F.; Spearman, J.G.; Lee, B.A.; Filice, G.A.; Holmes, K.K.; Griffiss, J.M. "Group A Meningococcal Disease in the U.S. Pacific Northwest: Epidemiology, Clinical Features, and Effect of a Vaccination Control Program," Rev Infect Dis. 1984, Sep.-Oct. 6(5). p. 640-648.

In 1975 an outbreak of group A meningococcal disease began in Seattle, Washington, and cases subsequently were recognized throughout the Pacific Northwest. Nearly one-half of the affected persons were Native Americans; two-thirds were alcohol abusers and/or habitues of skid row communities. In Seattle, group

A meningococci colonized asymptomatic persons only if these individuals had contact with skid row (P = .006). The epidemic strain may have spread from American Indians in Manitoba, Canada. Traditional migration routes connect the two populations; asymptomatic American Indians on reservations in Washington carried group A meningococci. Vaccination programs were undertaken in four cities, but only after cases occurred. In Seattle, vaccination reached 80% of the target population and was associated with a significant decrease in incidence of the disease, but cases recurred after the program ended. The social habits of skid row communities, combined with the "case-triggering" approach to and premature termination of vaccination programs, may have resulted in 56% of regional cases occurring after the start of the vaccination program in Seattle. Author.

Garber, J.M. "Corneal Curvature in the Fetal Alcohol Syndrome: Preliminary Report," Journal of the American Optometric Association. 1982, Aug. 53(8). p. 641-644.

In a preliminary report of the ocular characteristics of the fetal alcohol syndrome, (FAS) 17 Southwestern Indian FAS children were examined for ocular care. Of the seventeen examined, twelve could be measured with keratometry. 100% had corneal curvature of 45.75 and greater with an average horizontal curvature of 47.55 diopters and an average vertical curvature of 49.35 diopters. Steep corneal curvature was found to be a consistent and major characteristic of the FAS children.

Goedde, H.W.; Agarwal, D.P.; Harada, S.; Meier-Tackmann, D; Ruogu, D.; Brenzle, U.; Kroeger, A. and Hussein, L. "Population Genetic Studies on Aldehyde Dehydrogenase Isozyme Deficiency and Alcohol Sensitivity," American Journal of Human Genetics, 1983, 35(4), p 769-772.

Confirms previous findings of ALOH I deficiency and sensitivity to alcohol in Orientals but not South American Indians.

Hymbaugh, K.J., "Pilot Project on Fetal Alcohol Syndrome Among American Indians," Alcohol Health and Research World, 7(2): 3-9, 1983.

This article describes a comprehensive program designed to study and deal with the problem of fetal alcohol syndrome among Indians in the southwester United States. Training and education, clinical diagnosis and

treatment, and research and prevention are all components of this project. Each part of the project has
been designed to allow for a variety of complementary
efforts. 19 Ref.

Johnson, K.G. "Fetal Alcohol Syndrome: Rhinorrhea,
Persistent Otitis Media, Choanal Stenosis, Hypoplastic
Sphenoids and Ethmoid," Rocky Mountain Medical Journal,
76(2): 64-65, 1979.

A case report is provided of an Indian infant with
fetal alcohol syndrome (FAS) presented with heretofore
unreported symptoms. It is suggested that persistent
rhinorrhea, continuing otitis media, choanal stenosis,
and hypoplastic ethmoid and sphenoids be included as
possible manifestations of FAS. Similarly, FAS should
be added to the differential diagnosis of persistent
rhinorrhea, choanal stenosis, and/or otitis media
during infancy. 18 Ref.

Kleinfeld, J., Bloom, J.D., and Weed, V. "Using
Physiological Symptoms to Detect Psychological
Disturbances in an Eskimo Population," White Cloud
Journal of American Indian Mental Health, 2(4): 9-17,
1982.

It is suggested that physiological symptoms may be
useful as indicators of psychiatric disturbances in an
Eskimo village population, and that particular symptoms
with psychiatric significance may differ cross-
culturally. In this study, the authors examined the
potential of various symptom items of the Health
Opinion Survey (HOS) to measure psychological
disturbances in such a population. Responses of 70
Eskimos (42 males and 28 females) who were hospitalized
for psychiatric disorders (including alcoholism) were
compared with responses of 25 village Eskimos, obtained
20 years earlier. It was found that, on 9 of 18 HOS,
the hospitalized Eskimos had significantly higher
levels of psychiatric symptoms. It is concluded that,
in studies of psychiatric epidemiology in an Eskimo
population, a revised form of the HOS may be a useful
research tool; however, it should be used in
combination with other kinds of indicators which can
detect different forms of disturbances, and which are
perhaps more sensitive to certain population groups,
such as young Eskimo men. 14 Ref.

Lahey, B.B.; Kazdin, A.E.; eds. Advances in Clinical
Child Psychology. Vol. 9. Plenum Publishing Corp.,
New York, NY., 1986, 402 p.

Contents include chapters on psychopathology and its

antecedents among American Indian adolescents and on fetal alcohol syndrome.

McShane, Damian, Willenbring, Mark L.   "Differences in Cerebral Asymmetries Related to Drinking history and Ethnicity: A Computerized Axial Tomography (CAT) Scan Study," Journal of Nervous and Mental Disease,   1984, Sept. vol. 172(9) 529-532.

Examined normal computerized axial tomography scans of 50 American Indian, 60 black, and 60 white SS for cerebral asymmetry patterns, and information concerning the drinking history of each S was also obtained to examine differences in SS' cerebral asymmetries as related to their drinking history and ethnicity. Results indicate that alcohol-use history was associated with differences in asymmetry patterns, above and beyond differences associated with ethnicity. In SS without a history of alcohol use, more whites were likely to have left asymmetry of both occipital length and width as compared to American Indian and blacks. In SS with a history of alcohol use, all SS closely resembled one another, regardless of ethnicity. In the total sample, alcohol users were more likely to show greater right occipital width. 11 Ref.

Middaugh, J.P. "Serogroup A Meningococcal Meningitis in Alaska," Alaska Medicine, 23(6): 70-72, 1981.

An outbreak of serogroup-A meningococcal meningitis among the alcoholic, skid row population in Alaska is described, and measures instituted to control the outbreak are discussed. During 1976 and 1977, 32 cases of Group A meningococcal meningitis occurred in Alaska after 20 years with none reported. This outbreak coincided with outbreaks of Group A meningococcal disease in the skid row communities of Seattle, Washington and Portland, Oregon. Alaska adult skid row natives with a history of heavy alcohol use constituted most of the early cases and had an estimated annual attack rate of 1250 per 100,000, 625 times the state average. A limited Group A meningococcal vaccination campaign was directed at the alcoholic communities in Anchorage and Fairbanks, but the disease spread to other groups, particularly native children. Public health nurses vaccinated all persons at the city detoxification centers, and vaccine was administered in bars frequented by the high risk group. No adverse side-effects of the vaccination were identified. Since December, 1977, only two cases of Group A meningococcal disease are known to have occurred in Alaska. 14 Ref.

New Breast, T.   "American Indians at Higher Risk of Fetal Alcohol Syndrome," Conference Paper.   109th

Annual Meeting of the American Public Health Association.

The problem of fetal alcohol syndrome (FAS) and the American Indian population is discussed. Two nationwide FAS prevention programs are described. These are (1) the Indian Children's Program, supported by the Indian Health Service, and serving the Navajo, Apache, Ute, and 19 Pueblo tribes; and (2) the California Urban Indian Health Council's Fetal Alcohol Syndrome Program. 8 Ref.

Petit, C. "Drinking and Pregnancy," San Francisco Chronicle. San Francisco, CA: 27 Jul 1982.

The author cites some statistics on the fetal alcohol syndrome, and describes the efforts of Theda New Breast, director of the Fetal Alcohol Syndrome Prevention Program, sponsored by the California Urban Indian Health Council of Oakland, to convince other Indian women to stop drinking during pregnancy.

Rex, D.K.; Boyron, W.F.; Smialek, J.E; Li, T.K. "Alcohol and Aldehyde Dehydrogenase Isoenzymes in North American Indians," Alcoholism (NY). 1985, Mar.-Apr. 9(2). p. 147-152.

Alcohol dehydrogenase (ADH) and aldehyde dehydrogenase (ALDH) isoenzyme phenotypes were determined in autopsy liver samples from 50 North American Indians from New Mexico. Forty-six of the 50 livers has sufficient ADH activity to allow phenotyping at the ADH2 and ADH3 loci. All 46 livers possessed the "typical" ADH2 1-1 phenotype. The frequency of the ADH3 (2) allele was 0.59 and is the highest reported so far in any racial population. All 50 livers possessed the ALDH I isoenzyme which exhibits the greatest anodic mobility on starch gel electrophoresis at pH 7.6. The results show that ADH and ALDH phenotypes among American Indians living in New Mexico are very similar to those of Caucasian populations and quite different from those of Orientals. Author.

Schuckit, M.A. "Theory of Alcohol and Drug Abuse: A Genetic Approach," Theories on Drug Abuse, Washington, DC: Government Printing Office, 1980. 488 p. (pp. 297-302).

The author contends that genetically influenced biological factors explain only one part of the variance in the development of alcoholism and drug abuse, i. e., even for those persons genetically predisposed, the final clinical picture involves a combination of genetic factors (leading both toward and

away from substance abuse), and environmental events
(with similar positive and negative aspects).   Data
supporting genetics in alcoholism and other drug abuse
are presented and discussed.   Special problems
encountered in studying the genetics of alcohol and
drug abuse, and racial and ethnic populations
(including Native Americans) are discussed.

Smith, D.F. et al. "Intrinsic Defects in the Fetal
Alcohol Syndrome: Studies on 76 Cases from British
Columbia and the Yukon Territory," Neurobehavioral
Toxicology and Teratology, 3(2): 145-152, 1981.

A study of intrinsic defects in 76 fetal alcohol
syndrome (FAS) cases from British Columbia and the
Yukon Territory (Canada) is described.

Children diagnosed as FAS using standard criteria of
maternal alcoholism, poor growth, delayed development,
and characteristic facial appearance underwent an
investigative protocol involving pyleograms (IVP).
Significant skeletal findings included cervical spine
fusion in 20 of 46 children, x-ray confirmation of
microcephaly in 26 of 49 children, and abnormal
thoracic cage development in 13 of 48 children.
Thirty-nine of 54 children demonstrated a
characteristic tapering of the shaft and occasional
associated prominence of the tuft of the distal
phalanges.   Bone age was delayed 2 standard deviations
or greater in 14 of 51 children.   Cardiac lesions were
found in 31 of 76 children, and a further 12 children
had functional murmurs.   Lesions observed were
ventricular septal defect--20 cases, tetralogy of
Fallot--4 cases, plus a variety of less frequent
abnormalities.   IVPs were limited to 19 random cases,
with 5 cases showing alterations from the normal.
Cervical spine abnormalities of FAS were compared with
those of the Klippel-Feil syndrome.   Hand and lateral
cervical spine X-ray studies are a useful adjunct to
the diagnosis and management of the FAS.   23 Ref.

United States.   Indian Health Service.   Outline
Training Curriculum: Fetal Alcohol Syndrome.
Rockville, Md., date unknown, 7 p.

The clinical aspects of the fetal alcohol syndrome
(FAS) are described, including central nervous system
damage and physical abnormalities.   The etiology and
prevention of FAS, as well as where to turn for help
are also discussed.

United States Indian Health Service.   Bibliography on
Fetal Alcohol Syndrome and Related Issues.   Second
Edition.   Rockville, Md., 1981.

The bibliography on Fetal Alcohol Syndrome presents 312 unannotated journal articles for use by professionals working with American Indian people and is designed to serve as a vital source of knowledge on alcohol and child health. The bibliography is intended articles on Fetal Alcohol Syndrome and humans, and only highlight a minimal number on the effects of alcohol on experimental animals. The literature, from 1967 to 1980, includes topics such as the effects of alcohol on the fetus; alcoholism during pregnancy; smoking and drug addiction related to an infant's health; cases and history of Fetal Alcohol Syndrome; infants of alcoholic mothers; warning label views; prevention of Fetal Alcohol Syndrome; congenital malformations in offspring of alcoholic mothers; clinical perspectives on the Fetal alcohol syndrome; infants of drug addicted mothers; characteristics of the mental development of children of alcoholic mothers; effects of maternal alcohol, nicotine, and caffeine use during pregnancy on infant mental and motor development; psychologic handicaps in children with Fetal Alcohol Syndrome; and IQ in children of recovered alcoholic mothers. The bibliography also includes citations on experimental animals with Fetal Alcohol Syndrome.

Wallace, H.M. "The Health of American Indian Children," American Journal of Diseases of Children. 125(3), 1973, pp. 449-454.

This essay presents a summary and discussion of the health status of major health problems concerning American Indian Children of 1973. Included are discussions of demographic information relevant to health, birth rate, mortality rate for both infants and children, illness among children, nutrition in Indian children, mental health, and more recent health problems of youth, including school dropouts, juvenile delinquency, out-of-wedlock pregnancy, drug abuse, and venereal disease. Although the author notes that progress has been made, she also reports that these children are a "high-risk" group," in need of the delivery of health and related services.

Zeiner, A.R. "Are Differences in the Disulfiram-Alcohol Reaction the Basis of Racial Differences in Biological Sensitivity to Ethanol?" In: A. Schecter, Ed., Drug Dependence and Alcoholism, Vol. Biomedical Issues.

Research on the disulfiram-alcohol reaction and biological sensitivity to alcohol is reviewed. Physiological reactions to alcohol or alcohol and disulfiram include facial flushing, increases in heart rate, decreases in blood pressure, increases in skin conductance and in the frequency of nonspecific

responses.   The data indicate that the size of the
physiological reaction correlates strongly with blood
or breath acetaldehyde concentrations.   These findings
suggest that the biological sensitivity to ethanol
observed in some individuals and in some racial groups
may be related to acetaldehyde concentrations.   Several
factors involved in acetaldehyde production and
sensitivity vary with individuals and race including
differential   absorption   of   ethanol,   metabolic
differences associated with atypical liver enzymes, and
differences in organ sensitivity to acetaldehyde.   19
Ref.

3

CRIME

Bloom, J.D.   "Forensic Psychiatric Evaluation of Alaska Native Homicide Offenders," International Journal of Law and Psychiatry. 3: 163-171, 1980.

Characteristics of 30 Alaska natives (2 women) referred for psychiatric evaluation following indictment for homicide were compared with 27 nonnative Alaskan homicide offenders (4 women) also referred for psychiatric evaluation. Alcoholism was the most frequent psychiatric diagnosis made of the offenders. The typical offender was a single man, poorly educated, poorly skilled, and underemployed. Eighty-three percent of the native offenders consumed alcohol, in most cases quite heavily, at the time of the homicide. Fifty-six percent of the nonnative subjects used alcohol at the time of the homicides. Ninety percent of the natives and 59 percent of the nonnatives had a prior history of alcoholism or episodic abuse. Forty percent of the natives and 11 percent of the nonnatives had a past history of alcoholism treatment.

Bolton, Ralph, et al., "The Hypoglycemia-Aggression Hypothesis: Debate versus Research," Current Anthropology. 1984, 25, 1, Feb., 1-28.

A response to Ted Lewellen's critical evaluation of Ralph Bolton's work on the relationship between hypoglycemia and aggression among the Qolla of Peru. Lewellen ("Aggression and Hypoglycemia in the Andes: Another Look at the Evidence," Current Anthropology, 1981, 22, 347-361) argues that the Qolla are not highly aggressive, that they have been victims of stereo-typing and prejudice, that they are not especially prone to problems in glucose homeostasis, and that whatever aggression they display can largely be explained by their alcohol consumption....

Fischler, R.S.   "Child Abuse and Neglect in American Indian Communities," Child Abuse and Neglect. 1985. 9(1). p 95-106.

Child abuse and neglect have recently been found to occur among American Indians at rates comparable to other American population groups. Little is known about the clinical spectrum of Indian maltreatment, the psychodynamics and effective treatment modalities. Cultural misunderstanding, modernization, poverty, situational stress, poor parenting skills because of early break-up of Indian families, alcoholism, unusual perceptions of children, handicapped children, and divorce constitute factors associated with maltreatment in cases cited. Old solutions of removing children from families were largely inappropriate and ineffective and are being replaced by local efforts to develop foster homes, supportive family services, and legal procedures to protect children. Communication between agencies involved and mistrust of outsiders plus a lack of trained personnel and available community resources continue to pose major barriers to effective treatment and prevention efforts. Recent federal policies and laws clearly place the responsibility for child welfare in the hands of Indian tribes and tribal courts. The non-Indian health porfessional has an important but limited role in providing technical expertise and in aiding development of community resources, taking care to support but not usurp the emerging leadership of Indian people. Author.

Forslund, Morris A. A Self-Concept Comparison of Indian and Anglo Delinquency in Wyoming, Laramie, Wyoming: Governor's Planning Committee on Criminal Administration, 1974, 15 p.

The study is a continuation of previous research into the nature and magnitude of the delinquency problem among Wind River Indian Reservation youths in Wyoming. The study is based on responses to a self-report questionnaire concerning delinquent acts, alcohol use and drug use which was administered to students in grades 9-12 in high schools in the Wind River Indian Reservation area (May, 1972). Findings were based on a sample that included 335 Anglo males, 315 Anglo females, 68 Indian males, and 62 Indian females. There was little overall difference in the self-reported delinquent activities of Indian and Anglo males, with the exception that Indians were more involved in offenses centering around the school. Data did indicate, however, that compared to the Anglo female, the Indian female was considerably more involved in running away from home and in school centered offenses.

Also, although there was an indication of slightly greater drug use by Indians, the study did not indicate that illegal drinking is a greater problem among Indians than Anglos. The Indian youths in this study were disproportionately concentrated in the lower class and were somewhat underrepresented in the middle class. Thus, it is possible that some or all of the differences that have been found between Indian and Anglo delinquency may be due to differential social class distribution. This hypothesis was analyzed by sex, race, and social class.

Forslund, Morris A.; Meyers, Ralph E. "Delinquency Among Wind River Indian Reservation Youth," American Indian Law Review. 2, 1974, pp. 61-69.

The purpose of this study is to add to the knowledge of Indian delinquency through an investigation of the magnitude and dimensions of the delinquency problems among the Wind River Reservation Youth in Wyoming. The data obtained was limited to those that could be abstracted from official records of law enforcement agencies in the area. For the most part the findings confirm those of previous studies. The delinquency rate of the reservation youth is relatively high compared to that of the general American population. However, a high proportion of the charges are for minor offenses and alcohol-related offenses. What is now needed, the study indicates, is more intensive investigation into the similarities and differences between Indian and Non-Indian delinquency and the etiology of Indian delinquency.

Gilbert, J.N. "Police Training Needs of the Choctaw Indians, Mississippi Band," Ph.D. Dissertation, University of Southern Mississippi, 1985, 116 p.

The Police Division of the Choctaw Indians, Mississippi Band, was studied to determine their training needs in the priority areas of criminal investigation, patrol procedure, law and community relations. Data was gathered utilizing three investigative methods, a training needs questionnaire, semi-structured interviews, and crime index analysis. The survey instrument used the Likert scale to measure respondents' attitudes using a bipolar response. Responses were reviewed by frequency of percentage, singularly and by priority grouping. Officials who exercised administrative control over police operations were interviewed. Choctaw felony index crimes were compared with seven reservations of similar populations, allowing a progressive ranking by severity of crime. The results of the study indicated that a formal program of police training is needed within the

Police Division.   Officers and administrators perceived
the priority area of criminal investigation as having
the greatest training need.   Additionally, alcohol and
mental health problems were determined to be unique
areas of training need to the reservation environment.
Overall, the Choctaw reservation's crime rate compared
favorable to other reservations of similar population.

Harrell, Andrew W.   "The Effects of Alcohol Use and
Offender Remorsefulness on Sentencing Decisions,"
Journal of Applied Social Psychology,   1981, Jan.-Feb.,
vol. 11(1) 83-91.

Presentence reports on 628 offenders were content
analyzed.   Regression analysis found that remorseful SS
received less severe sentences than nonremorseful SS.
SS convicted of minor offenses received more lenient
sentences if they had used alcohol in conjunction with
their crimes than if they did not use alcohol.   The
opposite was the case for SS committing serious crimes.
Remorseful SS with few prior alcohol-related
convictions received less severe sanctioning than
nonremorseful SS with similar conviction records.   In
contrast, recidivists who were remorseful were dealt
with more harshly than their nonremorseful
counterparts.   37 Ref.

Jilek, Wolfgang, G.; Chunilal, Roy.   "Homicide
Committed by Canadian Indians and Non-Indians,"
International Journal of Offender Therapy and
Comparative Criminology.   1976, 20, 3, 201-216.

In British Columbia the homicide rate of Indians was
ten times higher than the general population of that
area; in the United States the Indian homicide rate is
estimated at three times higher.   Study of problems
associated with Indian homicide death in the United
States show that alcohol abuse is most prominent,
although no cause-effect relationship is postulated.
In 1975 and 1975, records were studies of those
convicted of criminal homicide in two British Columbia
federal corrections institutions, and each inmate was
interviewed.   Twenty-two native-born Indians were
matched with English-speaking Caucasian, Canadian-born
inmates.   Data on each group (social and family status
and history, cultural background, criminal record, and
"attitudinal variables") were compared between groups
and analyzed within the Indian group.   Six further
hypotheses, resulting from findings were proposed and
included that the Canadian Indians were
"overrepresented" especially in the area of
manslaughter, they shared different "attitudinal
variables" than Caucasians, and they showed less
psychotic or sexually deviant behavior.   4 Tables.

Long, Kathleen A.   "Cultural Considerations in the
Assessment and Treatment of Intrafamilial Abuse,"
American Journal of Orthopsychiatry. 1986, Jan. Vol.
56(1) 131-136.

Discusses the effect that cultural and subcultural
factors can have on reporting, assessing, and treating
abuse and family violence. Values and beliefs
associated with three specific rural situations--small
towns, Native American reservations, and cliques of
health professionals-- are examined, and four case
illustrations are presented. Case studies included (1)
An eight-year-old girl living on an Indian reservation
who had been severely abused by her alcoholic mother,
(2) A thirteen-year-old daughter of a prominent surgeon
who reported an incidence of sexual abuse by her
father, (3) A seven-year-old girl who was raped by her
uncle, and (4) a nine-year-old boy who was reportedly
molested by a neighbor. Recommendations are offered
for refining assessment and treatment strategies in
these settings. (8 Ref).

Marshall, Kaplan, Gans, and Kahn. Oglala Sioux Model
Reservation Program: Law and Order.   Volume 8,
Washington, D.C.: Bureau of Indian Affairs, 1969, 32 p.

The Oglala Sioux of the Pine Ridge Indian Reservation
suffer serious social disorganization, and hence a
large number of Sioux youth have had encounters with
the law. In this analysis of law and order on the
Sioux reservation, the authors contend that social
disorder has been caused by "inadequate misdirected,
and unresponsive public administration, and that the
Oglala Sioux have been encouraged and forced to act out
a role basically alien to their culture."   Thus,
protest does not take a constructive form, but rather,
a destructive one. Law and order therefore must be
responsive to the Oglala Sioux and to their cultural
values. Moreover, this report is concerned with the
formulation of a system of indigenous, responsive law
and law enforcement. The report recommends that the
law and order branch and the administration of justice
should become an instrument of community will--
responsive to the needs of the Pine Ridge Oglala Sioux.
The vernacular system of justice should be
strengthened: to include training and recruitment of
judges and vernacular attorneys. A crime prevention
program should be predicated upon the removal of
antecedent conditions to criminal and/or anti-social
conduct. Further, the tribal court should work to
reform tribal court practices immediately. (GRT).

Olson, Kenneth R.; Carman, Roderick, S; Pasewark,
Richard A. "Correlates of Alcohol Arrests in a Rural

State," International Journal of the Addictions.
1978, vol. 13(3), 415-425.

Arrest and conviction rates for public intoxication,
driving while intoxicated, and liquor law violations
were correlated with population, population change,
liquor sales, number of law officers, Indian
population, and overall crime rate for 23 counties in
Wyoming. It is concluded that increased liquor sales,
but not arrest rates, were associated with population
increase. 15 Ref.

Phillips, M.R.; Inui, T.S. "The Interaction of Mental
Illness, Criminal Behavior and Culture: Native Alaskan
Mentally Ill Criminal Offenders," Cultural Medicine
Psychiatry. 1986, June. 10(2). p.123-149.

The rapid changes experienced by non-Western ethnic
groups as they become "acculturated" to Western life-
styles are frequently associated with disintegration of
the traditional cultures and psychosocial dysfunction
of the groups' members. How culture changes lead to
maladaptation remains a mystery. As a first step in
clarifying this relationship, this paper proposes a
method for analyzing the interaction of cultural change
and psychosocial maladjustment. It uses Native
Alaskans as a paradigmatic example of a group that is
undergoing rapid changes and describes in detail a
maladjusted subgroup of Native Alaskans--mentally ill
criminal offenders. It compares 567 Native Alaskan
criminal offenders who were to mental health
professionals (from 1977 thru 1981) to 939 white
Alaskan offenders. We find that alcohol abuse, the
dominant social problem for native Alaskans, is not
clearly associated with the degree of sociocultural
change. Residence in larger communities and higher
educational achievement are associated with greater
psychosocial maladjustment. The region of residence
(i.e., Native Corporation) has a stronger influence on
the rate and type of maladjustment than the ethnic
group (i.e., Eskimo, Indian, or Aleut) or the "ethnic
density" of the community of residence (i.e., the
proportion of Native Alaskans in the population). We
emphasize the importance of using such quantitative
findings to focus the questions that should be
addressed by ethnographic research.

Schaefer, R. White Lightning and the Redman: American
Indian Arrest Rates for Alcohol-Related Offenses,
Macomb, IL.: Western Illinois University, Department
of Sociology, 1973, 17 p.

FBI Arrest statistics from 1934 to 1971 serve to
reinforce the image of the "Drunken Redman." Early

data (pre 1951) reflected a growing proportion of
Indian arrests related to alcohol usage. Indications
of the subsequent years point to a stable, though still
high, proportion of Indian arrests involving liquor in
urban and rural areas. Adolescent Indians in
comparison to their non-Indian peers were much more
prone to police encounters concerning the use of
alcohol. Police/civilian encounters as measured by
reported arrests reinforced the image of Indian
reliance on liquor and this reinforcement was
particularly strong in urban areas. Some possible
explanations (such as the prevalence of public versus
private places) are advanced to explain the relative
disparity while others (such as low income) are
questioned. 22 Ref.

Underhill, Ruth M., ed. Youth Problems on Indian
Reservations. Washington, D.C.: Department of Health,
Education and Welfare, Social and Rehabilitation
Service, 1970, 73p.

Juvenile delinquency was identified as the major
problem affecting youth on Indian reservations. Causes
for delinquency which were discussed included culture
conflict, expectation of failure, unemployment, failure
of homes and parents, discrimination, inadequate
education, off-reservation schools, and alcoholism.
Needs identified by tribal leaders included new
services and facilities for delinquent reservation
youth, training programs, and legal change for more
effective handling of juveniles. Progress was reported
in the areas of foster care, local involvement,
alternatives to incarceration, and recreational
programs. Inter-tribal cooperation, youth involvement,
and leadership exercised in the form of concrete action
were seen as essential to reducing delinquency among
reservation youth. Consultants described programs,
service organizations, and opportunities for Indian
youth. A conference agenda and lists of tribal
representatives and other participants are appended.

United States Bureau of Indian Affairs. The Combined
Tribal and Bureau Law Enforcement Services. Annual
Report 1972. Washington, D.C.: Bureau of Indian
Affairs, Division of Law Enforcement Services, 1972,
136 p.

This report provides a nationwide view of crime among
Indians, and is based on the reports of Indian law
enforcement agencies. While the level of crime clearly
rose over the three-year period 1970-1972, the cause of
these crimes vary significantly between reservations.
Thus, "The reader of this publication is cautioned
against comparing statistical information solely based

on a similarity in their population counts." The
report is divided into sixteen sections, the first and
most detailed of which specifies the trends in (and
geographic distribution of) those crimes used to
establish the index in the uniform crime reporting
program - murder, forcible rape, robbery, aggravated
assault, burglary, larceny $50.00 and over in value,
and auto theft. Each of these is discussed separately
in terms of volume, trend, rate/risk level, nature of
offense, clearances, persons arrested, and persons
charged. Subsequent sections of the report cover: (2)
offenses reported to police, (3) unfounded offenses,
(4) actual offenses, (5) offenses solved by arrests,
(6) arrests, (7) persons formally charged and
disposition. (8) persons granted probation, (9) traffic
accidents, (10) non-enforcement services, (11) Indian
court civil case report. (12) jail facilities, (13)
prisoner population, (14) offenses involving
intoxicating liquor/drugs, (15) vehicles assigned law
enforcement services, and (16) mileage traveled.
Throughout, statistical totals are provided via a
variety of formats (tables, pie graphs, bar-graphs,
graphs by time, etc.).

United States. Bureau of Indian Affairs, Division of
Law Enforcement Services, Law Enforcement Services
Annual Report 1976. Washington, D.C.: 1976, 58p.

This report, the last published under the old system of
crime reporting (extensive hand written reports),
provides a nationwide view of crime in Indian country.
During this period, the BIA was responsible for
providing law enforcement services on 126 Indian
reservations covering a total land area of
approximately 200,000 square miles. The report is
divided into sixteen sections, maintaining the form
(while considerably shortening the detail and length)
of previous annual reports in this series. The first
(and most detailed) section of the report specifies the
trends in (and geographic distribution of) those crimes
used to establish an index in the uniform crime
reporting program - murder, forcible rape, robbery,
aggravated assault, burglary, larceny-theft, and auto
theft. Each of these is discussed separately in terms
of volume, trend, rate/risk level, nature of offenses,
clearances, persons arrested, and persons charged.
Subsequent sections of the report cover: (2) offenses
reported, (3) unfounded offenses, (4) actual offenses,
(5) offenses solved by arrests, (6) arrests, (7)
persons formally charged and dispositions, (8) persons
granted probation, (9) traffic accidents, (1)) non-
enforcement services (11) Indian court civil case
report, (12) jail facilities, (13) prisoner population,
(14) offenses involving intoxicating liquor/drugs,

(15)   vehicles assigned law enforcement services, and
(16) miles traveled.

United States. Indian Health Service.   Indian Health
Service Training Center, Training Course TC-70-3:   A
Descriptive Study of the Academic Achievement,
Delinquency and Alcohol Usage of the Teenage Population
of the Reno-Sparks Indian Colony. Rockville, Md, 1970,
41 p.

In an effort to help define significant behavior
problems existing among Reno-Sparks Indian (Nevada)
teenagers, and to provide training in descriptive
epidemiology, a study group undertook an investigation
of demographic background, educational status, history
of juvenile delinquency, and history of personal or
family alcohol abuse among the study population.   It
was found that although the dropout·rate was high, it
was lower than the US all-Indian rate.   Unsuccessful
and early termination of education was related to
absenteeism, low achievement, and delinquency and not
related to crowded home conditions, family stability,
or income level.   Forty percent of the teenagers had
been arrested, some several times.   Alcohol use was
associated with many of the arrests and dropouts.
Recommendations for programs to address the problem
areas identified are offered.   5 Ref.

Wolf, Aron, S.   "Alcohol and Violence in the Alaskan
Native: A Follow-up and Theoretical Considerations,"
Alcoholism Treatment Quarterly,   1984, Spr. Vol. 1(1),
133-138.

Provides a follow-up discussion and theoretical
considerations concerning the present author's (1980)
case studies of alcohol blackout and homicide in
Alaskan natives.   Since that time, 10 more protocols
have been established, and other relevant cases have
been evaluated.   Congruent with the previous research,
it is demonstrated that alcoholic blackout is a
syndrome that stems from damage and destruction of
midbrain cells that are located in the medial thalamus,
the hypothalamus, and red nucleus.   When these cells
are destroyed, there is no macromolecular coding of
incoming sensory impulses.   The Alaskan Native American
has a slower curve of utilization of alcohol and builds
a higher blood alcohol level than his/her non-native
counterpart.   Clinical data from approximately 100
cases shows that Native Americans, who are otherwise
healthy, exhibited the blackout syndrome early in their
drinking histories.   It is asserted that, during
blackout due to alcohol consumption, Native Americans

do not have conscious, cortical control of their emotional behavior and are potentially dangerous to themselves and others.   11 Ref.

4

ETIOLOGY

Alaska Native Health Board, Health Care Evaluation Projects, Project to Analyze Risk To Alcohol Abuse Among Alaskan Native Students, Anchorage, 1976, 10 p.

A questionnaire survey was conducted among Alaskan native high school students at the Mt. Edgecumbe Boarding School to determine possible alcohol abuse risk factors among school-age populations. The students were screened for the presence of any of 67 possible risk factors, and these data were correlated with subjective assessments of the student's alcohol abuse status. A cohort of alcohol abusers was identified and followed over time to establish their alcoholic histories, and this information was eventually correlated with their risk factor profiles. Aside from the discovery of an extremely high incidence of drinking problems among this population, 5 factors (i.e., questionnaire responses) highly predictive of either development of or continued freedom from problem drinking were isolated. 9 Ref.

Alaska Native Health Board, Adolescent Alcoholism: A Relationship to Other Mental Health Problems, Anchorage, 1976.

The relationship between alcoholism and other mental health problems was studied in a survey of native Alaskan high school students at the Mt. Edgecumbe Boarding School. No differences were found between slight and moderate-to-severe alcohol abusers for any of seven target problems, namely, homesickness, feelings of grief, feelings of isolation, reading disabilities, learning disabilities, negative feelings regarding physical appearance, and boredom. The only significant difference between alcohol abusers (as a single group) and nonabusers was in the higher incidence of boredom among the abusers. The implications of these data for the planning and implementation of programs of assistance for such students are discussed.   3 Ref.

Albaugh, B.; Albaugh, P.   "Alcoholism and Substance Sniffing Among the Cheyenne and Arapaho Indians of Oklahoma,"   International Journal of the Addictions. 1979 Oct.,   14(7). P. 1001-7.

Common determinants of alcoholism and substance sniffing are identified among the Cheyenne and Arapaho Indians of Oklahoma.   Computer correlations, interviews, and questionnaires provided data. Findings indicate chronic sniffing is prealcoholic behavior. Confusing family interpersonal relationships, alcoholism in the immediate family, and severe parent-child emotional deprivation predispose to alcoholism. Author.

Andre, James M.,   Epidemiology of Alcoholism Among American Indians and Alaska Natives, Albuquerque, NM.: Indian Health Service, 1979.

Alcohol Abuse is described as the most widespread, severe, and all-encompassing health and social problem among American Indians today. The impact of alcohol abuse upon American Indian youth and upon American Indians are presented in two categories: mortality and morbidity. In the overall data for all areas and tribes served by the Indian Health Services, five of the top ten causes of death among Indian people are directly related to alcohol abuse: accidents; cirrhosis of the liver; alcoholism; suicide; and homicide.   These five causes are briefly discussed. The causes of morbidity which are directly related to alcohol abuse but do not immediately (but often eventually) result in death are listed.   It is concluded that the statistics should be viewed in the context of a people who are already beset with problems of racism, poverty, and powerlessness.

Apostle, R., and Miller, V. P.   Alcohol Consumption Among North American Indians: Drinking Patterns, Associated Problems, and Possible Causes, Ottowa, Ontario, Canada: 1975, 25 p. Health and Welfare Canada, Research Bureau, Non-medical Use of Drugs Directorate.

The literature on drinking patterns, associated problems, and causes of alcohol abuse among native Americans is reviewed in order to formulate some general statements on the subject and to suggest directions for future research. It is contended that despite the apparent lack of alcohol addiction, the heavy drinking which occurs among American Indians poses a number of social problems at the individual, family, and community levels. According to the author, future research of alcohol abuse among North American Indians must take into account the Indians' own points of view and opinions, particularly when it comes to attempts at reducing the amount of drinking. It is also suggested that without early education of Indian youth to the dangers of alcohol abuse and the accompanying provision of community facilities on the reserves to occupy the spare time of the youth profitably, alcohol abuse and its associated problems will continue.

Austin, Gregory A.; Johnson, Bruce D.; Carroll, Eleanor E.; Letteri, Dan J., Drugs and Minorities. Rockville, Md.: National Institute on Drug Abuse, 1977, 210 p.

An examination of research reports that deal specifically with minority drug use.

Barbor, T.F., Ed. Alcohol and Culture: Comparative Perspectives From Europe and America. New York: Academic Sciences, 1986, 239 p.

Contents Include: (selected) ethnic and antional differences in the manifestation and meaning of alcoholism: ethnic religions difference in the manifestation and treatment of alcoholism. Patterns of alcohol and drug abuse in drug treatment clients from different ethnic backgrounds. Drinking patterns among black and Nonblack adolescents--results of a national survey. Cultural factors in the etiology of alcoholism --a prospectus study. Alcohol treatment in American Indian populations--an indigenous treatment modality compared with traditional approaches. Cultural affiliation among American Indian alcoholics-- correlations and change over a ten-year period. Treatment and recovery in alcoholism contrast between results in white men and those in special populations. Implications for research and prevention policy: The public health perspective on alcoholism.

Chafetz, Morris E. "Problem of Alcoholism in the United States," International Symposium on Alcoholism and Drug Addiction. Zagreb, Yugoslavia: 1, Oct., 1971. 10p.

Included in this paper is a discussion of alcoholism among American Indians.

Couture, J.E. "The Socio-cultural Approach," In Addictions: What is Their Treatment? Proceedings of a Conference. Ottawa: Commoners' Publishing, 1981, 216 p. (pp. 27-49).

The etiology of alcoholism and problem drinking is discussed while exploring the sociocultural approach to the treatment of addiction among American Indians. Physiological, emotional, mental, and sociocultural causal components constitute alcoholism; compulsiveness is a distinguishing feature. The discussion includes cross-cultural analyses, studies of Native Americans and some current Indian-initiated efforts to deal with problem drinking.

Edwards, E. Daniel and Edwards, Margie E. "Alcoholism Prevention/Treatment and Native American Youth: A Community Approach," Journal of Drug Issues, future issue, 1988.

This paper addresses prevention, education, and treatment approaches for combating problems of alcohol abuse with American Indian children, adolescents and their families. Community involvement is emphasized. Included are primary prevention interventions which promote alternative activities to drinking while emphasizing positive feelings of self-esteem and identity. Also recommended are secondary prevention alcoholism programs which provide information regarding alcohol while encouraging responsible decision-making regarding drinking behaviors. Additional suggestions identify resources which can be made available to Indian youth who are developing problem drinking behaviors. A task group approach is recommended for identifying problem drinking behaviors in specific communities and developing viable programs to address these needs.

Estes, N. J.; Smith-DiJulio, K.; Heinemann, M. E. "Alcohol Problems in Special Groups: Racial and Ethnic Groups, Adolescents, Multidrug Abusers," Nursing Diagnosis of the Alcoholic Person, St. Louis: C. V. Mosby, 1980, vol. ix. 251 p (pp 46-72).

Expanding the appraisal process for those in special groups is discussed. The special groups discussed here included blacks, American Indians and Alaskan Natives, Asian Americans, adolescents and multi-drug abusers. For each group, the causative factors leading to drinking were presented along with the consequences of drinking. Special findings for each group were described and approaches in appraisal were suggested and implications for prevention and treatment were included. 54 Ref.

Estes, N.J., Heinemann, M.E. Alcoholism: Development Consequences, and Interventions, 2nd ed. St. Louis, Mo: C. V. Mosby, 1982, 385 p.

Research papers covering a broad spectrum of alcohol-
related subjects are presented under the following
general chapter topics: (1) developmental perspectives
of alcoholism; (2) pathophysiological effects of
alcohol; (3) alcohol problems in special groups; and
(4) therapeutic approaches to alcoholism. Chapter 18
by Joan Roper is entitled "Alcoholism and the American
Indian" (pp. 194-203).

Gomberg, E. L. "Special Populations," Alcohol,
Science and Society Revisited, Ann Arbor, MI.
University of Michigan Press, 1982. 440 pages. (pp.
337-354).

The author contends that the definition of "special
populations," i.e., those groups who have special
treatment needs and who have been underserved,
represents some real progress, recognizing the
complexities of alcohol problems; although the
differentiations made among alcoholics in Alcohol,
Science and Society (published in 1945), are valid and
important, the recognition of unique issues relating to
alcoholics in different age, racial, and gender groups
is useful and good. In this chapter, literature is
cited in a discussion of the diagnostic features of
alcoholism and social class differences used to
classify special populations (young, elderly, women,
and minority groups). A brief summative description of
the state of knowledge about the drinking patterns and
problems of each of these groups is presented. It is
concluded that a great deal more information is needed
about the drinking customs and social use of alcohol in
these special populations to develop effective
alcoholism prevention approaches. 34 Ref.

Heath, Dwight B.; Waddell, Jack O.; and Topper, Martin
D., eds., Cultural Factors in Alcohol Research and
Treatment of Drinking Problems. New Brunswick., NJ:
Journal of Studies on Alcohol, Inc., Suppl. No. 9,
January, 1981, 264 p.

This special issue contains several articles on Native
American alcoholism, including articles by Jack O.
Waddell, Robert K. Thomas, Jerrold E. Levy and Stephen
J. Kunitz, James M. Schaefer, Susan M. Stevens, Louise
Jikek-Aall, Wolfgang G. Jekek, and R. Dale Walker.
Other articles are on Hispanic alcoholism, black
alcoholism, and sociocultural contents of alcoholism in
general.

Jessor, R. "Adolescent Problem Drinking: Psychosocial
Aspects and Developmental Outcomes," In: Leland H.
Towle (Ed.) Proceedings: NIAAA-WHO Collaborating

Center Designation Meeting and Alcohol Research
Seminar,   Washington, D.C: 31 Oct. - Nov. 1983,
(pp.104-143, 1985z).

Research using high school and college youth samples,
adolescents from a tri-ethnic American Indian
reservation, and young people of southern Italian
lineage in Boston and Italy is reviewed. A conceptual
framework called the Problem-Behavior Theory is
employed here to examine three major sources of
psychosocial variation: the Personality System, the
Perceived Environment System, and the Behavior System.
These systems, when combined, are said to provide an
estimate of proneness to engage in problem behavior.
Data from a longitudinal study begun in 1969 on young
people in a Rocky Mountain city indicated that problem
drinking in the 16 to 18 year-olds in 1972 involved one
in four men and one in six women... Using multiple
regression analysis, the concepts of Problem-Behavior
Theory were found to be significantly correlated with
problem-drinking behavior... The findings indicate that
having been an adolescent problem drinker does not
predict becoming a problem-drinking young adult...
Proneness to problem behavior did predict problem
drinking 7 to 9 years later, especially for males.
Using this measure in individual prediction, however,
is discouraged. It is concluded that proneness to
adolescent drinking problems represents a pattern of
personality, environmental, and behavioral attributes.
Thus, prevention efforts should approach all these
areas simultaneously...A three dimensional model for
health promotion is discussed. It involves the
physical, psychological, social, and personal domains
of health; the personality, environmental, and
behavioral foci of intervention; and two strategies of
health promotion among adolescents: strengthening
health-enhancing behavior and weakening health-
compromising behavior. 16 Ref.

Jones-Saumty, D.; Hochhgas, L.; Dru, R.; Zeiner, R.
"Psychological Factors of Familial Alcoholism in
American Indians and Caucasians," Journal of Clinical
Psychology. 39(5): 783-790, 1983.

The familial factor and its relationship to the
transmission or risk of alcoholism in a group of
American Indians was studied. American Indians run
twice the risk of becoming alcoholics as the general
population.   In two related investigations,
psychological adjustment and drinking behavior were
assessed: (1) for a group of Indians with one or more
first-degree alcoholic relatives and a group of Indians
without a history of familial alcoholism, and 92) for
Indians with a history of familial alcoholism compared

to Caucasians with a history of familial alcoholism. Results indicated no psychological functioning differences between familial and nonfamilial Indians. However, the familial Indian group reported a style of drinking that more closely resembled that of an alcoholics group. Cross-cultural examination of these data reveal differences between Indians and Caucasians on psychological adjustment, as well as drinking behavior. These differences were present despite a shared familial history of alcoholism. 29 Ref.

Journal of Drug Issues, 14(2), Spring, 1984. Special issue on "Adolescent Drug Use," 436 p.

This special issue contains a fine piece by Joan Weibel-Orlando, "Substance Abuse Among American Indian Youth: A Continuing Crisis," Other articles in this issue are on substance abuse and Mexican-American Youth, black family features and drinking behavior, and on substance abuse and youth in general.

Kearns, B. "Commentary (to the Socio-cultural Approach)," In: Addictions: What is Their Treatment? Proceedings of a Conference. Ottawa Commoners' Publishing, 1981, 216 p. (pp. 60-67).

Couture's sociocultural approach to treatment of addictions is discussed (see Abst. No. 43, 1982) focusing on the cultural problem faced by Anglo-Saxon researchers when they work with Native American subjects who do not subscribe to the time and money-oriented culture of the researchers. Indian organizations themselves sometimes repeat the mistakes of the researchers. Cultural differences among various groups of Indians compound the problems. The need for cultural identification and restructuring among researchers is stressed.

Kim, Vivian C. List of Publications on American Indians/Alaskan Natives, Asian/Pacific Americans, Blacks and Hispanics Resulting from ADAMHA-Supported Research on Minorities 1972-1981. Rockville, Md.: Alcohol, Drug Abuse, and Mental Health Administration, 1984, 95 p.

Leatham, Raymond C. Report on the Etiology of American Indian/Alaskan Native Alcoholism and an Evaluation of the National Institute on Alcohol Abuse and Alcoholism Supported American Indian/Alaskan Native Alcoholism Projects. Rockville, Md., 1978, 30p.

An official NIAAA report is presented which focuses on American Indian/Alaskan native Alcoholism, and evaluates government and American Indian/Alaskan native

projects established to deal with the problem. The
report is divided into four parts: 1) historical
background relevant to the American Indian/Alaskan
Native alcoholism effort; 2) the unique special
relationship between the federal government and
American Indian/Alaskan Natives; 3) etiology - a review
of the current state of knowledge; and 4) an assessment
and evaluation of the effectiveness of NIAAA programs.
In an effort to develop methods to deal with the
alcoholism problem, a majority of Indian projects have
instituted culturally-oriented components. They are
intended to create and strengthen a positive identity
within the traditional American Indian/Alaskan Native
cultural base. Taking into account existing
conditions, the federal system will increasingly seek
ways to enable Indians to Administer, operate and
control these programs and services now being
administered by federal and other agencies. Data
indicate that the heaviest and most aggressive public
drinking can be found among Indian societies at the
family and band level of cultural integration. These
groups were most often hunters and gatherers. However,
while various statistics may apply to the entire United
States Indian population, one must be careful not to
apply these notions to specific tribes or parts of
tribes. Upon review of the current data, programs and
legislation, it is concluded that the existing NIAAA
Indian alcoholism programs are evidence that Indian
people have, in partnership with NIAAA, made great
strides in successfully combating alcoholism.

Lewis, R.G. "Alcoholism, and the Native American: A
Review of the Literature," In: Alcohol and Health
Monograph No.4: Special Population Issues.
Washington, D.C.: National Institute on Alcohol and
Alcoholism, 1982, 446 p. (pp. 315 - 328).

The author contends that, although alcohol abuse among
Native Americans (American Indians and Native Alaskans)
is well documented, little of that documentation is
either sound or substantive. To develop a fundamental
understanding of drinking patterns among Native
Americans, the unique relationship between the Native
American and the federal government is examined.
Literature on the cause of alcoholism and problem
drinking among this population is reviewed. The
incidence and prevalence of alcohol use is described,
and a critical discussion of treatment and future
trends is presented. Alcohol problems among Native
Alaskans are also discussed. It is concluded that
native Americans continue to be caught in a search for
identity and renewed pride, and are entering a
tumultuous transition period; social problems
encountered by this population must be addressed before

substantial progress can be accomplished in changing their drinking patterns.

Mail, P.D.   "American Indian Alcoholism: What is Not Being Done," Conference Paper, 110th Annual Meeting of the American Public Health Association.   Montreal, Canada: 15, Nov., 1982. 42p.

The author contends that, in spite of the somewhat intensive scrutiny to which American Indians and Alaska natives have been subjected over the years, a review of the alcohol literature continues to reveal areas which have not been explored or reported.   Literature is cited in a discussion of the following questions: (1) who are the experts who write about Indian drinking? (2) where has the drinking problem been studied and believed to exist? (3) what are the major theories about Indian drinking? (4) what is the real problem regarding Indian drinking which concerns professionals and community members? (5) what solutions to the Indian drinking problem have been disseminated? and (6) what needs to be done to construct a more comprehensive and complete scenario of not only the problem, but its solutions? 18 Ref.

National Indian Health Board Publishers. NIHB Health Reporter, Denver, Colorado/ 1602 S. Parker Rd., Suite 200/ Denver, Colorado   80231.

This valuable publication is one of the best ways of monitoring developments in respect to legislation and other activities concerning alcohol and Native American youth, and related health and mental problems.

North, Robert and Orange, Jr., Richard Teenage Drinking: The #1 Drug Threat to Young People Today. New York: Collier Books, Div. of Macmillan Publ. Co., Inc., 1980, 144 p.

This book does not contain much material on Native American youth alcoholism, per se.   But there are a number of areas that this book covers that would be of use.   Unfortunately, this book contains no index.

Oetting,   E.R.,   Edwards,   R.   "Reliability   and Discriminant Validity of the Children's Drug-use Survey," Psychological Reports, 56(3): 751-756, 1985.

A survey of drug use by children in grades 4,5, and 6 was developed and tested in two groups.   One sample consisted of 111 boys and 102 girls in a mid-size community (9 - 12 years old).   The other sample consisted of Native American children living on reservations.   In this sample there were 646 boys and

741 girls (also 9 - 12 years old). The survey assessed involvement with alcohol, marijuana, inhalants, and pills and included experimental psychosocial items. It is short, easy to read, and constructed so that it does not encourage drug use. The drug-use items were found to have high reliability and discriminant validity. It is concluded here that the scales possess adequate reliability for use in as low a grade as the fourth grade and should be useful for studying drug involvement in both minority and non-minority youth. 10 Ref.

Reid, J. "Opening Remarks on Native Evaluation," Conference paper. 2nd Annual Meeting of the Special Interest Group on Program Evaluation, Canadian Addiction Foundation. Regina, Canada: 8-9, Sept., 1982. 184 p. (pp. 149-151).

The evaluation of the National Native Alcohol and Drug Abuse program (NNADAPP) in Canada is briefly discussed. The problems associated with such an evaluation are noted, in particular, how Indian people have not been consulted or involved in the evaluation process, its design and timing. It is reported that Indian people in Saskatchewan recognize the need for and benefits of NNADAP, and are willing to accept program evaluation, providing they have significant input and control throughout the process.

Rhoades, Everett. "Alcoholism: One of the Top Killers,' Rhoades Says," Wassaja. vol. 9, Sept.-Oct., 1982. p 11(1).

Richard, R. "Commentary (to the Socio-cultural Approach)," In: Addictions: What is Their Treatment? Proceedings of a Conference. Ottawa: Commoners' Publishing, 1981, 216 p. (pp. 50-57).

The sociocultural approach to the treatment of addictions is considered in the context of the native Indian communities in Quebec. In addition to three hospitals, there are two social service centers. The chiefs of each community are responsible for establishing rules governing the use of alcohol in the villages, but the emergency rooms of the hospitals are full of cases of alcohol misuse and related injuries to men, women and children. The problems faced by the hospital staff are discussed from the sociocultural perspective, especially problems with child placement, the emergence of the nuclear family and alcoholism and gas sniffing among the very young, who return from the southern regions with newly acquired addictions.

Schaefer, J.M. "Firewater Myths Revisited: Review of Findings and Some New Directions," Journal of Studies on Alcohol. Suppl. No. 9:99-117, 1981.

Findings from research studies on the rates of ethanol
metabolism and disappearance in various racial and
ethnic groups are compared. Research is cited in a
discussion of alcohol sensitivity, i.e., the unpleasant
or pleasant effects of alcohol, among these groups.
Problems associated with general population studies in
determining genetic factors of the etiology of
alcoholism are also discussed. A valid genetic
framework for examining major etiological factors of
alcoholism is needed, but to provide such a framework,
culturally sensitive pilot studies need to begin. One
implication of this research direction is that
therapists, patients, and the general public should be
aware that the "firewater" myth may be mistaken. 75
Ref.

Shirt, P.   "Commentary (to the Socio-cultural
Approach)," In: Addictions: What is Their Treatment?
Proceedings of a Conference. Ottawa: Commoners'
Publishing, 1981, 216 p. (pp. 58-59).

Almost all deaths of Alberta Indians are alcohol-
related; very few die of natural causes. The work done
in British Columbia for preventing problem drinking
among the Indians and the cultural basis of treatment
are noted.

The Alcohol and Drug Problems Association of North
America. Selected Papers Presented at the General
Sessions Twenty Second Annual Meeting September 12 to
17, 1971, Hartford, Connecticut. Washington, D.C.,
1971.

Selected papers on a variety of alcohol-related issues
are presented, including alcohol use and alcoholism
among youth, women, and American Indians.

Thomas, R.K. "History of North American Indian Alcohol
Use as a Community-based Phenomenon," Journal of
Studies on Alcohol. Suppl. No. 9:29-39, 1981.

The historical use of alcohol by North American Indians
is examined from a community-based perspective. An
explanation for the origin of excessive drinking among
Native Americans is provided, including descriptions of
the various types of heavy drinkers among this
population. The recent tendency for heavy drinking to
produce what is believed to be an increased dislocation
among Indian societies is discussed.

United States. American Indian Policy Review
Commission. Task Force Eleven. Report on Alcohol and

Drug Abuse: Final Report to the American Indian Policy Review Commission / Task Force Eleven: Alcohol and Drug Abuse. Washington: U.S. Govt. Printing Office, 1976, 97 p.

United States Indian Health Service. Alcoholism: <u>A High Priority Health Problem: A Report of the Indian Health Service Task Force on Alcoholism</u>. Rockville, Md., 1974, 19p.

This guide contains definitions of common words used in books and papers on alcoholism, short descriptions of a few of the modern methods of treatment and a list of organizations and agencies that can provide information or consultation on alcoholism. It was written to help tribal council persons, health board members, community health representatives and other members of Indian communities become better informed on alcoholism and to inform them of the action needed to prevent or control it.

United States Indian Health Service. Alcoholism: <u>A High Priority Health Problem - Section Two</u>. Rockville, Md., 1970.

This guide provides a balanced view of comprehensive alcohol treatment for the individual and the broader community aspects such as education, training, planning, and program development. It is intended as a brief outline of the way in which a service unit might operate in an Indian community. Each Indian community is unique and requires assessment of local mores and resources before a workable program can be developed.

United States Indian Health Service. Alcoholism: <u>A High Priority Health Problem- Section One</u>. Rockville, Md., 1969.

An effective alcoholism prevention and control program for the American Indian requires some understanding of the roots and causes of the various manifestations of harmful drinking. Alcohol is a means of coping with feelings of anger, frustration, and boredom which the American Indian experiences today. Their lack of education, meaningful employment, status, and economic autonomy create feelings of inferiority which can lead to an onset of drinking. Adult men and youth of both sexes are particularly affected.

United States Indian Health Service. Indian Health Statistics: Chart Series. Rockville, Md., 1979, 72 p.

This report is a compilation of tables and charts with brief annotations on the health status of American

Indians and Alaska Natives, 1977, with trends for selected years from 1955. Data are from the Indian health Service (IHS), with comparative U.S. data from NCHS and CDC. It contains thirty-five tables grouped in the following seven sections: births, mortality, and disease data show number of cases and/or rates with comparisons for the total U.S.:   A. program accomplishments, population and health indexes; 3 tables. B. birth; 2 tables. c. deaths, by cause; infant mortality, by age; mortality due to tuberculosis and gastrointestinal diseases; and maternal mortality; 8 tables. D. deaths from accidents, by cause and age; and from homicide, suicide, and alcoholism; 7 tables. E. health services utilization: IHS and contract hospital admissions and discharges, by diagnosis; and hospital and field clinic outpatient visits; 5 tables. F. disease incidence: otitis media, tuberculosis, trachoma, gonorrhea, and syphilis; 5 tables G. IHS hospitals, by year of construction; dental services provided; community health nursing visits, by IHS area and problem; Indian homes provided sanitary facilities; and medical cost trends; 5 tables.

United States Indian Health Service. Alcoholism--- A High Priority Health Problem. A Report of the Indian Health Service Task Force on Alcoholism. By George Bock, et al. Rockville, Md. 1972, 25 p.

Three separate reports are included in this document on American Indian Alcoholism. Section I of the document (December 1969) outlines the history, nature, extent, and significance of Indian alcoholism (reporting that the incidence of alcoholism among Indians is twice that of the national average, low socioeconomic status, rather than a physiological propensity, is cited as a major cause). Section II (February 1970) addresses the problems of alcoholism prevention,control and treatment (direct personal services via both professionals outside the community and nonprofessionals within the community; thorough, coordinated training for those providing services to alcoholics and/or their families; major health education principles and methods; community relationships which utilize the Indian Health service as a catalyst for program development; the importance of data collection, research and evaluation in any alcoholism program; and a suggested approach to program planning, including 12 specific recommendations). Section III (April 1970) is a reference guide to alcoholism programs and resources (includes a glossary of common words used in literature on alcoholism, short descriptions of a few of the modern methods of alcoholism treatment, and a list of organizations and agencies which can provide information, consultation, and, in some cases, financial support for community alcoholism program development.

United States National Institute on Alcohol Abuse and Alcoholism. Alcohol and Health Monograph No. 4: Special Population Issues, Rockville, Md.; 1982, 446 p.

Research papers are presented on the unique problems of special population groups whose need for alcoholism and alcohol abuse programs has been underserved. It is stated that a base of scientific knowledge exists on prevalence, incidence, and nature of alcohol-related problems of special population groups, defined by sex, age, race, and ethnicity. Two chapters on Indian alcoholism are included (by R. Lewis and J. Weibel).

United States. National Institute on Alcohol Abuse and Alcoholism. Alcohol and health... Special Reports. Rockville, Md., 1971, 1974, 1978, 1981, 1984.

These special reports are issued periodically. The last report, issued in 1984, is officially entitled the Fifth Special Report on Alcohol and Health. These are invaluable sources for research on alcoholism in general, and Native American youth alcoholism.

United States. Office of Technology Assessment Indian Health Care: Summary, Washington, D.C., 1986, 55 p.

This report is "an assessment of health care for American Indians and Alaska Natives who are eligible for medical and health - related services from the Federal Government." (p.7). This report was prepared at the request of the House Committee on Energy and Commerce and its Subcommittee on Health and the Environment, which have legislative and oversight jurisdiction over all federal health programs that are funded through general revenues. Considering the fact that alcoholism is a major health problem in Indian America, it is surprising how little mention is given it here. Still, this is a good overview of Indian health care, that can be valuable in respect to researching alcohol problems and Indian youth.

Watts, Thomas D., "Alcohol and Native American Youth: An Historical Perspective," Paper delivered at the Mid-America Conference on History, September 13, 1986, University of Arkansas, Fayetteville, Arkansas.

This paper examines alcohol and Native American youth in an historical perspective, and is divided into the following periods: First, the period before 1832; Second, the period between 1832-1953 (Native American prohibition period) and, Third, 1953-present.

Watts, Thomas D. and Wright, Jr., Roosevelt, eds., Black Alcohol Abuse and Alcoholism: An Annotated Bibliography. New York: Praeger Publ., 1986, 265 p.

This annotated bibliography contains 24 references that refer to Native Americans (see page 261 under "Native Americans" in the Index). Many of the references feature comparative studies of Native Americans and other ethnic groups.

Wright, Jr., Roosevelt and Watts, Thomas D., guest editors, Journal of Drug Issues special issue on "Alcoholism Problems and Minority Youth." forthcoming, 1988.

Three articles in this special issue deal with Native American youth and alcohol. E. Daniel Edwards and Margie E. Edwards, "Alcohol Prevention/Treatment and Native American Youth: A Community Approach", Eugene R. Oetting, and Fred Beauvais and Ruth Edwards" Alcohol and Indian Youth: Social and Psychological Correlates and Prevention", and Thomas D. Watts and Ron Lewis "Alcoholism and Native American Youth: An Overview." Another article of possible assistance is Gerald Globetti, "Alcohol Education Programs and Minority Youth."

5

GENDER

Beauvais, F., Oetting, E.R., Edwards, R. "Boredom, Poor Self Image, Lead Young Indian Girl to Drugs" NIHB Health Reporter, 3 (2): 5-9, 1982.

The incidence of drug and alcohol abuse among young Indian people on many reservations is reportedly high. The experiences of an 11-year-old Alaskan Indian girl who uses drugs as a means of escape from problems and as a result of peer pressure from her friends are described.

Echohawk, M. "Views on Chemical Substance Abuse by American Indian Women" Conference paper, Bicultural Women's Forum, Center for multicultural Awareness Conference, Washington, DC: 23-25 Aug., 1979. 8 p.

Although adolescent Indian families do their share of experimenting with a variety of drugs, alcohol seems to be the most commonly used, or at least, the drug most often associated with serious social, economic, and health problems in the lives of Indian women. A National Institute on Drug Abuse definition of primary prevention is presented, and is utilized in this discussion, because it defines primary prevention as a "constructive process," which the author finds crucial regarding drug abuse among Indian women. Background information regarding an earlier prevention process encountered by Indian people which was not constructive is also presented. Religious, legislative, and educational systems, considered to have had the greatest influence on weakening tribal stability are described in relation to a present day value system for Indian women and drug abuse prevention strategies.

Forslund, M. A. "Drinking Problems of Native American and White Youth" Journal of Drug Education, Farmingdale, NY: 9: 21-27, 1979.

Among 683 9th-12th grade Wyoming High-school students, of whom 58 were American Indian boys, 311 white boys, 49 American Indian girls and 265 white girls, 85-90 percent indicated that they had drunk an alcoholic beverage during the past year. A very high percentage (81 percent of Indian and 93 percent of white boys, and 100 percent of Indian and 86 percent of white girls) reported they had done so when a parent or guardian was not present. A significantly higher (p .001) percentage of Indian than white boys, had passed out (43.1 vs 30 percent), and passed out more frequently, during the past year, and a significantly higher (p .001) percentage of Indian than white girls had felt high, been drunk (87.5 vs 71.2 percent), been sick passed out (39.6 vs 14 percent) or experienced a brief loss of memory as a result of drinking (48.3 vs 26.5 percent). Of the Indian boys and girls, 32 and 23 percent reported that they had been stopped by the police for driving under the influence during the past year, compared with 24 and 11 percent of their white counterparts. A higher proportion of Indian than white boys and girls (53 and 65 vs 42 and 27 percent) said they had been "In Trouble" with their parents as a result of drinking.

Galanter, M. (Ed.) Currents in Alcoholism: Recent Advances in Research and Treatment, Volume VII. , Bronx, NY.: Albert Einstein College of Medicine, Department of Psychiatry, 1980, 548 p.

Papers on recent advances in alcoholism research and treatment, presented at the Annual National Council on Alcoholism (NCA) Forum, held in Washington, DC., in May, 1979 are provided. This volume is divided into three sections: biomedical issues, psychological and treatment issues, and social and demographic issues. Each section is preceded by an overview and is divided into two or three parts. The parts themselves are preceded by instructions that address both the topic areas and the relationship of the papers in that part to the topic. This results in an integration of preclinical and clinical work as well as in a presentation of clinical issues in an interdisciplinary context. One of the topics covered here is Native American women.

Hurlburt, Graham and Gade, Eldon. "Personality Differences Between Native American and Caucasian Women Alcoholics: Implications for Alcoholism Counseling," White Cloud Journal. 1984 Vol 3(2) 35-39.

95 Native American female alcoholics were compared with 39 Caucasian female alcoholics, using the Eysenck Personality Questionnaire (EPQ), to explore

implications for more effective alcoholism counseling
with Native American women. SS were between 16 and 60
years of age. Approximately 75% of all SS were in
treatment for alcoholism or participated in Alcoholics
Anonymous (AA) chapters. Results show that Native
American SS were significantly higher on the toughmindedness scale and Caucasian SS. Native American SS
in extended treatment programs were also significantly
more extroverted than Caucasian alcoholics in this type
of program. Both Native American and Caucasian SS In
AA were more similar in personality measures to females
in the EPQ standardization group than were SS in
detoxification or extended treatment programs. The
need to translate personality differences between
Native American and Caucasian female alcoholics into
traditional and culture-specific alcoholism counseling
procedures is discussed. (14 Ref.).

Knipp, M.M.; Begishe, M. "Beliefs and Behavior of
Navajo Women Related to Alcohol Consumption" Research
in Progress. Rockville, Md., Indian Health Service,
date unknown.

Using an interview technique the authors will gather
data from Navajo women on the following subjects: 1) A
definition of problem drinking from a cultural context
and 2) ethnographic information on the role of drinking
in the live of the Navajo woman. The focus of the
research is on women of childbearing age due to the
prevalence of fetal alcohol syndrome (FAS) in the
population. Using the data obtained the authors hope
to identify general patterns and trends in the area as
well as areas for future research. LT

Swanson, D.W.; Bratrude, A.P.; Brown, E.M. "Alcohol
Abuse in a Population of Indian Children," Diseases of
the Nervous System. 32, 1971, pp. 835-842.

The pattern and course of severe alcohol abuse by 42
Indian children (22) females) is described. The main
reason given for drinking was boredom. Though the real
reason was more likely social acceptance by the group.
Most of the parents of these children were alcoholic
people, and some entire families were drinking
excessively. Beer was the beverage of choice. The
consequences of drinking were school dropout, sexual
promiscuity, illegitimate pregnancy, delinquency,
physical complications, and suicide. An incomplete
follow-up of the children and some additional data on
adult subjects indicate that such children usually
become alcoholic adults. Among many causes of
childhood abuse of alcohol, the most apparent is the
Indian respect for individual autonomy which combined
with permissiveness for other reasons, allows the child

to determine how much alcohol he will drink. Obvious in this traditional behavior is ignorance or denial of the fact that alcohol is a drug. The major etiologic factors in Indian alcoholism thus seem to be habituation and social acceptance. A four phase treatment program is proposed.

Webster, L. "Alcohol and Drug Abuse Among Indian Women and Youth in Wisconsin, Minnesota, and Michigan." "Working with Adolescent Alcohol Drug Problems: Assessment, Intervention and Treatment," Conference Paper.Madison, WI: 6-8 Feb, 1983. 135 pages (pp. 33-35).

The results of a study of 1136 Indian women and youth in Wisconsin, Minnesota, and Michigan regarding their alcohol and other drug experience are presented. The raw data contained 46 variables. The three major factors which were derived from these data are alcohol and drug abuse, self-concept, and an awareness factor. Of these three, the most important part of the survey was composed of questions examining the first, alcohol and drug abuse. It was found that 29 percent of those who said they used alcohol because of boredom also said they used alcohol more frequently than other respondents. Thirty-two percent of those completing the questionnaire made up excuses for alcohol use, 44 percent experienced guilt feelings after drinking, and 40 percent of those using alcohol frequently experienced blackouts. Additionally, it was discovered that 12 percent of the 10-12 year olds used drugs or alcohol enough to be considered abusers. About three percent of this age group indicated that they always used drugs or alcohol. As the levels of use predictably rise with age, 35 percent of the 13-15 year olds are users, and among 16-18 year olds, it is over 50 percent. A copy of the questionnaire survey used in this study is included.

Wilmore, M.A. "Alcoholic Women: Her Crisis and Her Recovery," Conference paper, Women in Crisis Conference, New York, NY.: 18 May 1979. 21 p.

The stigma against alcoholism which has closeted and possibly killed many female problem drinkers is being attacked by a variety of different forces in society. This paper is divided into two parts: (1) a profile of alcoholic women; and (2) treatment issues common to most alcoholic women. This paper depicts a composite of the experiences of women's treatment programs. Indian women are included here. 30 Ref.

Wilsnack, Sharon C. Drinking and Denial of Social Obligations Among Adolescent Boys, Grand Forks, ND:,

University of North Dakota School of Medicine, Department of Neuroscience, 1979. Also see Wilsnack, Richard W. and Wilsnack, Sharon C., "Drinking and Denial of Social Obligations Among Adolescent Boys," Journal of Studies on Alcohol, 41(11): 1118-1133, 1980.

A study was conducted to learn more about how specific orientations toward masculine role performance affect male drinking. Data were analyzed from a 1974 national survey on adolescent drinking. A two-stage stratified cluster sample was taken which included approximately 15,000 students in grades 7-12, in the contiguous 48 states plus the District of Columbia. Ethnic stratification of the 50 primary sampling units allowed oversampling of localities with high concentrations of Oriental, American Indian, and Spanish-American residents to insure that these minorities would be adequately represented. All students were asked to complete an anonymous, self-administered questionnaire, which included items on drinking behavior, contexts and consequences of drinking, deviant behavior, and selected demographic, attitudinal, and personality characteristics. It is concluded that denial of social obligations is a role-orientation more pronounced among boys and is linked to their drinking more heavily, with more adverse social consequences, and with more symptoms of alcohol dependence. Adolescent drinking as masculine role performance may be connected with deviant behavior and reduced social control, with drinking possibly used as part of a rebellion against authority and as a means of gaining "Time Out" from social responsibility.

6

POLICY AND PREVENTION

Alaska Native Health Board, Risk Analysis: A Concept
and Its Application to Alcoholism and Mental Health,
Anchorage, 1975, 12 p.

This report describes a project of the Alaska Native
Health Board aimed at establishing a set of factors for
both identifying school-age children at risk for
alcohol problems and for predicting the outcome of
specific therapeutic modalities. The project was based
on preliminary expert analysis and agreement on a list
of "Risk Factors" by which to compare each client
represented in a "Data Base for Alcohol Problems." The
state and degree of severity was then correlated with
the various risk factors. Initial findings provide
interesting data on factors which discriminate between
students with and without an alcohol problem. Risk
factor analysis is viewed as having great potential as
an aid in alcoholic client screening and evaluation and
in studies of the progression of alcoholism form one
stage of severity to another.

Andre, James M. Public Health Approach to the Primary
Prevention of Substance Abuse, Albuquerque, NM.:
Indian Health Service, 1979.

The public health prevention approach is presented as a
model for handling alcohol abuse among American Indian
and Alaska Native Youth. Three types of prevention are
identified. Primary prevention is the most desirable,
and consists of educational measures aimed at
strengthening the individual and family against
potentially stressful and harmful events. The
educational process which will diminish the attraction
of substance abuse includes: (1) values clarification,
(2) self-concept clarification, (3) decision making
techniques, (4) social interaction skills, (5) drug
education, and (6) parent effectiveness training.

Secondary prevention, aimed at early case findings and treatment and tertiary prevention, aimed at reducing impairment following a disease, are also reviewed in terms of their application to substance abuse.

Beauvais, F. Preventing Drug Abuse Among American Indian Young People, Fort Collins, CO.:   Colorado State University, Psychology Dept., 1980.

This report is intended for people who are in the field working with drug abuse problems among Indians, and is divided into three parts.   The first part is a summary of what is known about drug (including alcohol) abuse among Indian youngsters.   The second part describes things that can be done about drug abuse in Indian communities.   Some of these suggestions are based on research, while others are things that are already being done in some communities.   The third part contains descriptions of different kinds of drugs, and their effects on people.   30 Ref.

Beauvais, F.; LaBoueff, S.   "Drug and Alcohol Abuse Intervention in American Indian Communities," International Journal of the Addictions.   1985, January.   20(1). p 139-171.

American Indian tribes are seen as an anachronism by many non-Indian people.   Most would acknowledge that Indians provided a colorful chapter in American history, but apart from contemporary Indian arts and crafts little serious thought is given to their way of life.   In face, however, Indian culture has survived a period of strong attack and today it is vital and growing.   The historical conflicts between Indian and White ways of life are still not totally resolved, and there are major differences in thinking as to whether tribes should be assimilated into the larger culture or allowed to pursue an alternate cultural path.   In its ambivalence toward Indian people the federal government has fostered a state of dependency which has made problem resolution extremely difficult.   Federal policy has vacillated between paternalistic and repressive, which has let to much inertia within both Indian communities and those groups intended to help them. Currently there is a strong activist climate on Indian reservations and the result is a vigorous move toward self-determination.   Not only are Indian people asking for self-government, but they are attempting to revitalize their traditional culture and maintain a unique alternative to the beliefs, values, and customs of the larger society.   Within this historical/cultural context, drug and alcohol abuse exist as major problems for Indian people.   Extant data point to alcoholism as perhaps the number one health problem for many tribes.

The consequences of drug abuse are not as well documented, but recent survey data from Indian school students point to an extremely serious situation. Drug use rates are above national norms and appear to be rapidly increasing. Interventions in Indian communities must be congruent with the current movement toward self-determination. Externally imposed solutions, at a minimum, will not work and probably will only add to the sense of failure experienced by Indian people. The dynamics of drug and alcohol use are rooted in the health of the community. Where there is cynicism, despair, and a withering of the basic human spirit, substance abuse will prevail. Alternately, if the spirit of the community can be bolstered and hope developed through communal action and mutual support, solutions to abuse problems will be forth coming. When the community has clearly decided its position on the use of chemicals it will be in a position to construct programs and request external assistance. Substance abuse intervention is a local problem and can be resolved best through local initiative. 48 Refs.

Bellamy, G. R. "Policy Implications for Adolescent Deviance: The Case of Indian Alcohol Prohibition," Dissertation. John Hopkins University, Baltimore, MD. Dissertation. Abstracts International, 45(8): 2663A, 1985.

The hypothesis here was that Indian youth residing on reservations that retain prohibition laws will show greater deviance, both behavioral and attitudinal, than similar youth residing on reservations that have repealed prohibition. Three groups of Indian adolescents, grades seven through twelve, were given a self-administered survey. Each group represented a different legal response made to the 1953 Federal repeal of Indian prohibition. One group retained prohibition, one group repealed prohibition in 1953 and the third repealed in 1970. The results did not support the hypothesis. The results did indicate that differences in policy are associated with differences in adolescent deviance. The 1953 repeal group was significantly more involved in deviant behavior than similar youth in the 1970 repeal group, and the prohibition group fell

Blane, Howard T. and Chafetz, Morris, E., eds., Youth Alcohol, and Social Police I. New York: Plenum Press, 1979, 424 p.

There is little here on Native American alcoholism, per se. Nevertheless, the chapters contained herein contain much of interest to those researching Native

American youth alcoholism between the two. A further study of drinking behavior provided parallel results. Within each group, females were more socially conforming than their male counterparts, suggesting they are subject to more cultural constraints on their behavior.

Bergman, Robert   "The Human Cost of Removing Indian Children From Their Families," In: The Destruction of American Indian Families, Steven Unger, Ed., New York: Association on American Indian Affairs, 1977, pp. 34-36.

The purpose of this essay is to critique those federal programs and people who have attempted (and succeeded) for the past 100 years or so to remove Indian children from their families and from the "... influence of his savage parents," this is not the answer and only serves to increase the number of juvenile dropouts, underachievers, alcoholics, drug addicts and unsociables. The schools and homes to which these children are sent are unprepared to meet their needs. It is the author's opinion that the children would most often be better off "... if left with the parent or close relative. Therapy or counseling could be provided to these families." Rough Rock and Rock Point Schools on the Navajo Reservation are two excellent examples of good Indian schools and the Toyei Dormitory School is another good example. Indians should be allowed to develop their own standards for determining child placements as well as their own curriculum for schools, with consultation provided at their request only.

Best, Josefina E.   "Comparative Analysis Of Alcohol Abuse Among Two Ethnic Minority Groups," Dissertation. May 1979, 129 p.

The socio-cultural aspects of alcohol abuse among Native and Black Americans are compared. A review of literature is presented concerning alcohol abuse among teenagers and its implications for nursing practice. Teenage abuse was found to be widespread among both sexes, with parents, peers and television making a tremendous impact on the learning process. The author proposes a preventive alcohol education program for youth.

Briskin, A. S. Closing the Circle Again: A Drug Abuse Curriculum Written and Developed for the Minnesota Chippewa Tribe, St. Paul MN: Minnesota Department of Public Welfare, 1980, 400 p.

The wonders of the human body, the impact of alcohol

and drugs on the body's systems, and how to get high
naturally instead of chemically are discussed from the
viewpoint of the American Indian lifestyle.

Burns, Thomas R.   "An Application of Indian Health
Service Standards for Alcoholism Programs," White
Cloud Journal (3) 2, 1984, 26-34.

This article discusses Phoenix-area applications of
1981 Indian Health Service standards for alcoholism
programs.   Results of standard statistical techniques
note areas of deficiency through application of a one-
tailed Z test at .05 level of significance.   Factor
analysis sheds further light on design of standards.
Implications of revisions are suggested.

Carpenter, R.A., Lyons, C.A., Miller, W. R.   "Peer-
managed Self-control Program for Prevention of Alcohol
Abuse in American Indian High School   Students: A
Pilot Evaluation Study," International Journal of the
Addictions, 20(2): 299-310, 1985.

A peer managed self-control program designed to teach
responsible drinking was tested with 30 American Indian
teens at high risk for problem drinking. Students were
randomly assigned to three groups, each incorporating
combinations of self-monitoring, peer-assisted self-
control training, and alcohol education.   Significant
decreases were seen in quantity and frequency of
drinking in peak blood alcohol levels.   The
improvements were maintained at follow-ups of 4, 9, and
12 months after treatment.   Self-report data were
corroborated by breath tests and by official records.
No group differences were found which indicted that
minimal and full program interventions had comparable
effects.   35 Ref.

Cooley, C. Albuquerque Area Youth Advocacy Program with
Special Focus on Alcohol and Other Drug Abuse
Prevention, Albuquerque, NM.: Albuquerque Area Youth
Advocacy Program, 1980, 33 p.

It is stated that in order to develop any meaningful,
consistent and predictable program that will meet the
needs of youth in the Albuquerque, New Mexico area, a
redirection of program services must be effected.   The
author contends that the ultimate direction of a youth
advocacy program will depend on several issues which
range from administrative and financial considerations
to coordination and redefinition of the program
presently being offered.   Organizational goals and
management objectives, oriented toward the ultimate
direction and development of a comprehensive and
integrated youth advocacy program with a special focus

on alcohol and other drug abuse prevention, are presented.

Dru, R. L.   "Future Direction of Alcohol and DrugAbuse,"   Conference   paper,   4th   National Indian/Alaskan Native Health Conference, San Diego, CA: 9 Apr. 1981.   8 p.

Public health concepts of primary, secondary, and tertiary prevention of alcohol and drug abuse (substance abuse) are discussed.   Tasks of primary substance abuse prevention and specific action steps (primary and secondary prevention) are outlined.   A list   of   some   target   groups   and   examples   of technological information transfer are also provided. It is concluded that major prevention efforts must consist of effective primary prevention aimed at youth because: (1) they have yet to attain their full physical, emotional, and intellectual growth, i. e., they are more susceptible to the effects of drugs including alcohol; and (2) not only are youth the greatest resource for the future, but those who are substance abusers are at high risk of becoming tomorrow's problem adult.

Everett, Michael W.   Anthropological Expertise and the "Realities" of White Mountain Apache Adolescent Drinking.   Monograph, Supplement, Symposium on American Indian Drinking: Pathology or Perspective?" Lexington, Kentucky, Department of Anthropology, 1973, 43p.

Different anthropological research strategies are compared for efficacy in dealing with conflicting conceptual realities in the development of alcohol and mental health programs to meet the needs of the American Indian Community.   An ethnographic and conceptual perspective is contrasted with an objective, pathological one, with specific reference to the analysis of adolescent drinking behavior among the White Mountain Apache.   Finally, the appropriateness and usefulness of the anthropologist's contribution to Indian drinking programs, as judged by Indians, is considered.   25 Ref.

Globetti, Gerald   "Alcohol Education Programs and Minority Youth,"   Journal of Drug Issues,   future issue, 1988.

Research relative to the drinking behavior of minority youth, as well as alcohol abuse prevention programs for these youth, have been largely neglected.   Moreover, the existing data on both of these subjects are limited in that they either treat minority youth as a homogeneous entity or apply a white middle class curriculum to prevention activity. This paper examines several alcohol education protocols within schools and how these strategies present unique problems to prevention programs for minority youth. Curricula derived from the developmetnal and the socio-cultural models appear most applicable to minorities.

Helmick, Edward F., Mcclure, William T., Mitchell, Patricia M. "Project to Analyze Risk to Alcohol Among Alaskan Native Students," Currents In Alcoholism: Vol. 2, New York: Grune and Stratton, 1977, 565 p. (pp. 367-376).

Efforts of the Alaska Native Health Board, Mental Health Evaluation Project to identify individuals who might be at high risk in developing an alcohol problem are highlighted in this report. After consultation with 40 Alaskans, both providers and nonproviders, a list of 67 potential risk factors was developed. Subsequently, 359 adolescent students were tested against those factors. Evaluation of the initial test and alcoholism status by counselors revealed that 105 of the students were abusing alcohol. Students who had a drinking problem were found to be similar to those who had no drinking problem in age and sex characteristics. There were fewer women in the alcohol abuse group (33 percent) than in the normal group (43 percent). It is surmised that in spite of the small sample used in this study, generalization of methodology and utility is possible. 9 Ref.

"H.R. 4567 Amendments May Pave Way for New Indian Alcoholism Bill," NIHB Health Reporter 3(12): 5,12, 1984.

The bill considering the reauthorization of the Indian Health Care Improvement Act included amendments regarding the prevention of alcohol and drug abuse with the following provisions: (1) the Indian Health Service (IHS) and the Bureau of Indian Affairs will be required to compile existing studies and literature, including school curricula, relevant to juvenile Indian alcohol and drug abuse; (2) both departments will also be required to incorporate a training program for teachers, administrators, and counsellors in alcohol and drug abuse, and (3) The Office of Alcohol Programs within IHS will be provided funding for additional staff.

Manson, S. M., Tatum, E., Dinges, N. G. "Prevention Research Among American Indian and Alaska Native Communities: Charting Future Courses for Theory and Practice in Mental Health" In: S. M. Manson, Ed., New Directions in Prevention Among American Indian and

Alaska Native Communities. Portland, OR: Oregon Health Sciences University, 1982. 404 pages (pp. 11-64).

Various factors and conditions that have influenced the course of prevention research among American Indian and Alaskan Native communities are considered, and avenues along which this research might productively proceed in the future are explored. Concepts of prevention research are discussed, focusing on implications for those working in American Indian mental health. An overview of the literature on such research is presented. Some statistics on the nature and extent of alcohol and drug abuse among American Indian adults and youth are provided. It is suggested that the competent individual, community, and culture are useful guideposts by which to plan and pursue future prevention research in Indian mental health. It is argued that the ensuing focus more readily accommodates the discovery of strategies for achieving the goal of competent mental health promotion. 168 Ref.

Manson, S.M.; (ed.) New Directions in Prevention Among American Indian and Alaska Native Communities. Portland, Or.: Oregon Health Sciences University, 1982. 404p.

This monograph is the product of a planning workshop that was designed to focus on prevention concerns (including alcohol and drug abuse) related to American Indian and Alaska Native communities. The workshop was organized and sponsored by the National Institute of Mental Health (NIMH) Office of prevention in collaboration with the National Center for American Indian and Alaska Native Mental Health Research, and was held on 24 and 25 September 1981 at Timber Lodge, located near Portland, Oregon on Mount Hood. Papers are provided under the five workshop sections: research, training, services, program evaluation, and recommendations for prevention research planning.

Martin, G. L.; Ward, E. E.; Newman, I.M. Evaluation as a Part of Primary Prevention Programming: The Indian Youth Project, Lincoln, Nebraska: University of Nebraska, Nebraska Center for Alcohol and Drug Abuse, 1982.

Efforts that were made to increase the specificity and usefulness of evaluating a primary prevention program, the Indian Youth Program, are reported here. This program of the Lincoln (Nebraska) Indian Center had as one of its aims the improvement of interpersonal skills and abilities among its participating youth. The first year's activities in this program led to a refinement of the objectives and a concern among staff that they were not measuring the critical outcomes that were set forth in their program objectives.   A set of measurements are presented that were developed to better assess how well the program was actually meeting its stated goals.   Results indicated that the Indian Youth Program was effective in achieving its objective. The following items are appended:

(1) an outline of psychosocial development to be monitored; (2) the Indian Center staff training manual for behavior documentation; and (3) a behavior documentation chart.   5 Ref.

Mason, Velma Garcia and Baker, George   Growing Up and Feeling Powerful as an American Indian.   Rockville, Md.:   National Institute on Drug Abuse, 1978, 24 p.

May, P.A.   Alcohol and Drug Misuse Prevention Programs for American Indians: Needs and Opportunities," Journal of Studies on Alcohol.   1986, May.   47(3). p.187-195.

General statistics have indicated that the problem of alcohol and drug misuse among American Indians has been in need of attention for years.   A specific and critical examination of mortality and morbibity statistics yields a number of valuable insights to the ways of addressing the problem.   The current status in many communities dictates intervention at three levels. First, high mortality and morbidity rates must be reduced through creative and innovative intervention with social and physical environment.   Alcohol legalization and other issues are discussed as distince porribilities.   Second, educational porgrams are needed to elevate the knowledge of American Indian communities about alcohol and drug misuse.   Education should be specifically oriented to improving ability to deal with early developmental problems that might lead to misuse. Third, American Indian rehabilitation programs need to be upgraded and improved by gaining more resources and byusing them more effectively.   Increased use of both traditional tribal strengths and modern treatment modalities is promising.   Rehabilitation programs may be even more important in the future if mortality reduction programs such as those described are successful.

Maypole, D.E.; Anderson, R.   "Alcoholism Programs Serving Minorities: Administrative Structures and Problems,"   Conference paper.   National Council on Alcoholism Forum.   Houston, Tx.: 14-17   April, 1983. 18 p.

Findings from previous studies of alcoholism services provided to minorities are summarized. Preliminary findings are reported from a research project designed to study the delivery of services to minorities in an upper Midwestern State. Objectives of this study were to determine the unique administrative problems experienced by administrators of community alcoholism treatment agencies serving minorities, or minority administrators in agencies which served only majority clients, to examine the agency structures, and to recommend solutions to these problems. A summary description for each of the seven agencies studied is provided, and problem areas found within these agencies are described. Minority administrators' relationship problems are enumerated, and community program administrators' recommendations are presented, including the views of State agency administrators. Implications of these findings are discussed. 17 Ref.

Medicine, B. "New Roads to Coping - Siouan Sobriety," In. S.M. Manson, Ed., New Directions in Prevention Among American Indian and Alaskan Native Communities. Portland, Or.: Oregon health Sciences University, 1982. 404p. (pp. 189-213).

Ethnographic observation of drinking patterns and an awareness of the various ways in which the underlying cognitive dynamics may be expressed are critical to: (1) understanding the experiences of American Indian alcoholics, their achievement as well as maintenance of sobriety; and (2) formulating successful strategies for coping with the diverse pressures that initially contribute to alcoholism in Indian people. The tendencies toward and the maintenance of sobriety among individuals (Lakota Sioux) on the Standing Rock reservation (Iowa) who have learned to cope without the use of alcohol are delineated, focusing on the mechanism for this maintenance. 46 Ref.

Messolonghites, Louisa, Multicultural Perspectives on Drug Abuse and Its Prevention: A Resource Book, Rockville, MD.: National Institute on Drug Abuse, 1979.

This resource guide is divided into two sections. In the first section, "Perspectives", the types of drug and alcohol abuse associated with specific ethnic and social minorities in the U.S., and prevention efforts in multicultural communities are reviewed. In the second section, "Information and Education Resource Guide," available materials related to drug and alcohol abuse among cultural and ethnic groups as well as sources of information about this topic are listed.

Mohatt, G.; Blue, A.W.   "Primary Prevention as it Relates to Traditionality and Empirical Measures of Social Deviance," In: S.M. Manson, ed., New Directions in Prevention Among American Indian and Alaskan Native Communities. Portland, Or.: Oregon Health Sciences University, 1982. 404p. (pp. 91-118).

"Tiogpage" is a Sioux word that describes a community way of life which is patterned by Lakota Sioux rules for social interaction, rituals for transition, identity acquisition, and healing. A project that bears this name arose out of discussions held by an organization of Sioux medicine men, their helpers, and associates on a Northern Plains reservation. Propositions formulated by these leaders (called "wapiyawicage" or healers) are outlined, and results of a project designed to examine these propositions are presented. This project, conducted from 1978 through 1980, was funded by the Center for Minority Group Mental health Programs in the national Institute of Mental Health, and had the following three tasks: (1) to develop a way to measure the tiogpaye community as a style of life; (2) to discover if social and psychological distress, as measured by levels of various pathology indicators (including alcohol abuse), bears any relationship to the tiogpaye way of life; and (3) to implement a form of intervention that builds upon the tiogpaye way of life and to reduce such or, minimally forestall further increases in social and psychological distress. Findings indicate that residents of the Northern Plains, whether alcoholic or not, employed or unemployed, distressed or effectively coping, still subscribe to a very traditional lifestyle or live in a very traditional community. It is concluded that this situation is clearly a very complex interaction which researchers have just begun to explore; however, it must be conceded that traditionality does not appear to be the panacea for primary prevention that many people hope. 21 Ref.

Moore, Mark H. and Gerstein, Dean R., eds., Alcohol and Public Policy: Beyond the Shadow of Prohibition. Panel on Alternative Policies Affecting the Prevention of Alcohol Abuse and Alcoholism. Washington, D.C.: National Academy Press, 1981, 463 p.

This book is not on Native American youth alcoholism, per se. But it is an important study that may prove helpful in drawing implications for Native American youth alcoholism. The Panel on Alternative Policies Affecting the Prevention of Alcohol Abuse and Alcoholism was charged by its sponsor, the National Institute on Alcohol Abuse and Alcoholism, to produce a systematic analysis of alternative policies affecting the prevention of alcohol abuse and alcoholism.   This book is handicapped by not having an index of any kind. Nevertheless, it is an important study, with much to say on this seminal subject.

Morningstar, Incorporated, Morningstar Incorporated: An Experiential Learning Community, Billings, Montana: Bureau of Indian Affairs, 1976, 214 p.

The purpose of this study was to evaluate the effect of Morningstar, Incorporated, an Experiential learning community located in Billings, Montana. Results of the evaluation revealed many problems within the organization and personnel of the community, including personality conflict, political controversy, jealousies, etc., in addition, four major deficiencies were cited: (1) time spent on attacks concerning the program; (2) attempts to please all and finding that the program pleased none; (3)spreading the staff too thin; (4) loss of sight with regard to goals and objectives.   Rebuilding of the program was then discussed.   Included were topics such as training, follow-ups, youth and their activities.

Mosher, J.P.   "Alcohol Policy and the Nation's Youth," Journal of Public Health Policy.   6(3): 295-299, 1985.

The alcoholic beverage industry exploits the alcohol market by increasing availability, using price differentials (with low overall relative price), introducing new products, and engaging in intense promotional campaigns.   These techniques are coordinated to maintain and expand consumption.   This strategy ("total marketing") is discussed.   Public policy initiatives can be powerful tools in shaping youthful drinking patterns.   Several policy options, including increasing federal excise tax on alcoholic beverages and equalizing taxes on wine, beer and distilled spirits, are discussed.   Alcohol problems are community and social problems requiring a collective commitment to change.   Society must be willing to reexamine its drinking norms and expectations and to create healthy drinking environments before it can expect children to make informed choices regarding the use or nonuse of alcohol.

Multicultural Drug Abuse Prevention Resource Center. What Life Will We Make for our Children? Inglewood, CA., 1980, 21 p.

A Comprehensive perspective of native American drug (including alcohol) abuse and prevention as a community concern is presented in a discussion of the following five   major   aspects: (1)   drug   abuse   prevention strategies; (2) influences of society and culture on individuals; (3) conditions which contribute toward drug abuse; (4) role of an Indian community in drug abuse prevention; and (5) suggested processes and procedures for community involvement in drug abuse prevention.

Nelson, Leonard "Alcoholism In Zuni, New Mexico," Preventive Medicine, 6, 1977, pp. 152-166.

An investigation into the etiology and medical and social consequences of alcoholism among Zuni Indians in New Mexico revealed that alcohol is a major factor in Zuni mortality, especially among the young; and because multiple causes and modifying factors have made alcoholism a major health problem among the Zuni, the author proposes a community-based rehabilitation program in which many disciplines would pool their resources. Because many Zuni alcoholics believe that they are "Possessed," a unique feature of the center would be the pre sence of a full-time medicine man on the staff. Recent changes in familial roles are discussed, as well as the lack of recreation in Zuni. The police force, comprised of Zunis (many of whom drink frequently), have a poor understanding of alcoholism and often treat the alcoholic with brutality.

NIHB Health Reporter. "Indian Substance Abuse Provisions Included in Omnibus Antidrug Act," 4(5), part 1, January, 1987, pp. 1, 2, 4, (published by the National Indian Health Board).

This article discusses the Omnibus Drug Enforcement Education and Control Act of 1986, (P.L. 99-570) passed by the 99th U.S. Congress, and the inclusion of provisions for Indian alcohol and substance abuse prevention and treatment. The Indian provisions of the act "incorporate and expand on legislation directed at alcohol and drug abuse among Indian youth which had been considered earlier in the congressional session" (p. 1).

NIHB Health Reporter. "Indian Community Triumphs in Struggle Against Alcoholism," 4(5), part 1, January 1987, pp. 10-11 (published by the National Indian Health Board).

This article discusses the successful campaign against alcoholism of the Alkalai Lake Tribe of British Columbia, Canada (400 Shuswap Indians living in an area 300 miles northeast of Vancouver, British Columbia, Canada). This article, reprinted from the Lakota Times, described the efforts of Freddie Johnson,

Phyllis and Andy Chelsea and others in their successful struggle against alcoholism in the Alkalai Lake community.

Nutting, P.A.; Solomon, N.; Carney, J.P. "Health Care System of the Winnegago Tribe: Application of a Method to Assess System Performance for Alcoholism," Indian Health Service, Office of Research and Development, Rockville, Md.: 1980. 93 p.

Results are presented from a study designed to investigate the application of a method to assess health care system performance for alcoholism, in terms of both the processes and outcomes. This study was conducted jointly by the Office of Research and Development of the Indian Health Service (IHS) and the Health Department of the Winnebago Tribe of Nebraska, between April 1977 and April 1979. The study population consisted of 653 people (321 males and 332 females), 504 of whom were Indians and 149 non-Indians, residing on the Winnegago Indian Reservation. The process of care was determined by tracking these individuals through 8, 183 contact with components of the health care system and auditing the records of each individual within each of the twelve component health programs. Outcomes of care achieved were determined by assessing each individual's status with regard to alcoholism at both ends of the study time frame. Results indicate that the prevalence of alcoholism among the Indian community of Winnebago is approximately 39 percent compared to a prevalence of 8.2 percent among the non-Indian component of the community. It is concluded that this approach to health care evaluation is feasible and yields results which are useful in the management and modification of the health care systems. 8 Ref.

Nutting, P. A.; Price, T. B.; Baty, M. L. "Non-Health Professionals and the School-Age Child: Early Intervention For Behavioral Problems," Journal of School Health, 49: 73-78, 1979.

At a large American Indian boarding school, the efficacy of utilizing Title 1 (special education program) dormitory parents for early intervention in behavioral problems such as alcohol abuse was studied. Dormitory parents identified and assessed early manifestations of behavioral problems with the help of a 14-item checklist. Depending on problem severity, intervention included either informal individual counseling by the dormitory parent or referral to a professional counselor. Students were aged 17-18, about half were women and 4 cohorts were studies; i. e., Title I students in Title I and Non-title I dormitories in two consecutive academic years. Compared with the year previous to the intervention program, there was a decrease in the alcohol abuse rate and the mean monthly incidence of alcohol abuse (P.) 1 in both cases).

O'Connor, J. P., and Rosall, J. "Our Vision: A Journey to Better Health." Proceedings of the Third National Indian/Alaska Native Health Conference, Indian Health Board, Inc., Denver, CO.: 1979.

Proceedings of the Third National Indian/Alaska Native Health Conference, held on 22-26 July 1969 in Spokane, Washington, are presented. Alcohol abuse and alcoholism problems among Native Americans were discussed in legislative, human services, and mental health workshops. Conference resolutions are also presented.

Oetting, E.R.; Beauvais, Fred and Edwards, Ruth. "Alcohol and Indian Youth: Social and Psychological Correlates and Prevention," Journal of Drug Issues I, future issue, 1988.

Youth Native American childern (ages 12-16) who used alcohol heavily were compared with matched non-users. Alcohol users did not have more emotional problems. They experienced less alienation and felt as self-confident and socially accepted as non-users, but used other drugs and were more deviant. Alcohol users came more often from broken families and felt less family caring and fewer family sanctions against substance use. They had poorer school adjustment and less hope for the future. Friends of alcohol users encouraged alcohol and drug use and provided few sanctions against use. Prevention, for Indian youth, needs to start very early. Programs should focus on increasing family strength, improving school adjustment, porviding opportunities for the future, breaking up deviant peer clusters and building peer clusters that discourage alcohol and drug use.

Powless, David J. "National Native Alcohol Abuse Program Activities," Conference paper, Futuraction '77 Conference, Winnipeg, Manitoba, Canada: July 1977. 11 p.

The National Native Alcohol Abuse Program in Canada has four operative terms: Awareness, Prevention, Rehabilitation, and Spirituality. The incidence of alcoholism in various Indian reservations is discussed. The program stresses education of youth and the need for young people to obtain a sense of personal value and dignity.

Parades, Alfonso   "Social Control of Drinking Among the Aztec Indians of Mesoamerica," Journal of Studies on Alcohol. 1975, Sept. vol 36(9) 1139-1153.

Historical evidence suggests that the Aztec culture or pre-Columbian Mexico rules for the use of alcoholic beverages were clearly defined and strictly enforced. Drinking was permitted only on religious occasions and the amount consumed was restricted. (24 Ref.).

Raymond, M.P.; Raymond, E.V.   Identification and Assessment of Model Indian Health Service Alcoholism Projects. Rockville, Md.:   Indian Health Service, 1984, 159p.

The primary objectives of the study were to define conceptual models of several types of alcoholism treatment and prevention services, and to describe existing Indian Health Services Alcoholism Projects, components that fit the various models. Site visits were conducted to twelve programs that had been selected as examples of the following types of programs or components: Prevention/outreach, detoxification, primary residential treatment, halfway house, out-patient, and comprehensive. Models developed initially from the literature and comments of the Advisory panel were revised, as appropriate, based on information gained during the site visits. The contractor presented several recommendations which include testing of the models, training, and management of the program.

"Report On The Beer Distributors Of Indiana Inc's. Alcohol Abuse Program," Brewers Digest, 54(11):   38-39, 52, 1979.

A 13-minute film entitled "Booze and Yous" is the core of the alcohol education and prevention program developed by the beer distributors of Indiana, Inc. (BDI). The film, which was produced with a (BDI grant to the Indiana University Foundation, has been used by over 400 colleges and universities in alcohol education classes. Also, using the film as a catalyst for discussion, local beer distributors in Indiana state "Beer" parties (a beverage to enjoy and entertain responsibly) for civic groups and legislators in their communities. The program has developed both to inhibit public misuse of alcohol, particularly among youth, and to inhibit severe legislative action against beverage distributors and wholesalers.

Save the Children. Caring, Coping, Change: Challenges for the 80's. A Report of the National Indian Child Conference (4th, Albuquerque, New Mexico, September 12-16, 1982).

The report of the fourth National Indian Child
Conference (1982), sponsored by Save the Children,
contains a statistical portrait of the American Indian
child, synopses of 7 major presentations and 64
workshops recommendations, a conference evaluation, and
lists of conference staff, presenters, and tribal
representation. Topics of major presentations are
traditional Indian medicine; ways to teach children a
Native American perspective; microcomputers in
education; trends in education; Save the Children;
family day care; and leadership. Workshop topics
include self-esteem, creative writing, community
planning, cultural awareness/preservation, handicapped
children, suicide prevention, mental health programs,
parenting, bilingual education, adult education, child
abuse, fund raising, local school boards, teenage
pregnancy, preventative health education, early
childhood education, gifted children, and substance
abuse and therapy. Recommendations presented are for
increased funding for Indian Child Welfare Act
programs; improved communication between federal
agencies affecting Indian children; opposition to
closure of the Southwestern Indian Polytechnical
Institute and other Indian schools; dissemination of
information regarding the 1982 Indian Housing Act to
Indian communities; continues pre-kindergarten programs
through Indian Student Equalization Programs; increased
community involvement in planning preventative health
education curriculum school-age parenting classes and
child care in Indian communities; and encouraging use
of native foods through the schools.

Schinke, S.P., Gilchrist, L. D., Schilling, R. F. II,
Walker, R. D., Kirkham M. A., Bobo, J. K., Trimble, J.
E., Cvetkovich, G. T., Richardson, S. S. "Strategies
for Preventing Substance Abuse with American Indian
Youth." White Cloud Journal of American Indian Mental
Health.   3(14): 12-18, 1985.

Primary prevention is an appealing response to
substance abuse problems among American Indian people.
However, substance abuse prevention programs developed
with Indian people, based on empirical data and
oriented toward youth, have not been forthcoming.
Culturally sensitive, scientific strategies for closing
gaps in the substance abuse prevention research
literature are presented here. Strategies of
assesment, design, implementation, and evaluation in
the service of preventing substance abuse with American
Indian youth are described. The strategies are
discussed here relative to their advantages and limits.

Schinke, S.P., Schilling, R. F. II, Gilchrist, L.D.,
Barth, R. P., Bobo, J. K., Trimble, J. E., Cvetkovich,

G. T. "Preventing Substance Abuse with American Indian Youth." Social Casework: The Journal of Contemporary Social Work, 66(4): 213-217, 1985.

Prevention methods are discussed here based on theory and research and are intended to be used by groups on Indian youth, led by Indian social workers, teachers, and school counselors. The methods include providing information and changing attitudes, assisting with problem solving, designing coping statements, improving interpersonal communication, and organizing social networks. Possible implications for future substance abuse prevention efforts are discussed. 29 Ref.

Streit, Fred, and Nicolich, Mark J.   "Myths versus Data on American Indian Drug Abuse," Journal of Drug Education, 7(2):   117-122, 1977.

The prevalence of drug and alcohol use among 2,647 Montana Indian Youths, age 6 through 18, was surveyed in 1975.   Survey results indicated that approximately 50 percent of the children's fathers in this sample were dead, not living at home, or unemployed.   More Indian youth who have lived on a reservation and who speak or understand their Indian language were found to be users of alcohol and other drugs.   The children of unemployed fathers, who appeared to spend more time together, were less likely to use drugs.   There was no difference in alcohol use, although a negative attitude to both alcohol and drugs was found in this group.   It is concluded that research and evaluation findings from other cultures do not apply to the American Indian. More research into the differences and needs of this population is called for to obtain effective prevention programming.

Trimble, J. E.   "Drug Abuse Prevention Research Needs among American Indians and Alaska Natives." White Cloud Journal of American Indian Mental Health 3(3): 22-34, 1984.

The need for well researched methods to prevent substance abuse and to reduce its incidence among American Indians and Alaskan Natives especially among young people, is discussed here.   Drinking among American Indians has been associated with anxiety, dependency, powerlessness, hostility, stress, and acculturation pressures.   Some theories suggest that American Indians rapidly metabolize ethanol, that they are hypersensitive to the effects of alcohol, and that they are genetically unprepared to drink in moderation. It is concluded that substance abuse prevention research for American Indians and Alaskan Natives will require the following organizational and institutional arrangements: (1) the support of Indian-oriented applications through a separate pool of resources, such as an ad hoc initial review group consisting of competent ethnic minority researchers to deal with the research and service oriented applications; (2) inclusion of American Indians and Alaskan Natives, through their own representatives, in the planning, implementation, and dissemination of substance abuse prevention research activities in their communities; (3) convention of a series of conferences to pursue issues specific to American Indians and encourage interagency collaboration in this effort; (4) establishment of regional substance abuse and development centers; (5) involvement of American Indians and Alaskan Natives in the cataloging, abstracting, and dissemination of the final reports of substance abuse prevention projects; and (6) inclusion of Indian oriented professional associations, such as the National Indian Health Board, the American Indian Physicians Association, the special committee in Indian Affairs within the American Psychiatric Association and the National Center for American Indian Mental Health Research in the planning and dissemination of substance research activities. 89 Ref.

Trimble, J. E. "American Indian Mental Health and the Role of Training for Prevention," New Directions in Prevention Among American Indian and Alaska Native Communities, Portland, OR: Oregon Health Sciences University, 1982, 404 p. (pp. 147-171).

The training of people to work effectively in the area of mental illness prevention is discussed, specifically as this training relates to working with and in Indian communities to promote positive mental health and to develop programs which prevent social and individual disruptive and destructive behavior. These two themes incorporate aspects of sometimes clashing philosophical orientations, i. e., the present-day, conventional culturally encapsulated approaches to prevention as opposed to training, cultural, and tribal-specific orientations. It is reported that: (1) alcohol and drug abuse is considered to be the number one mental health problem among Indians, with survey results indicating that the alcohol abuse rate is greater for Indian youth than other groups; and (2) while alcohol prevention efforts targeted for youth alone are meager in comparison to programs for individuals at other developmental stages, the efforts to prevent such abuse are even fewer for American Indian youth. Suggestions for future programmatic development in training American Indians and non-Indians to work in the field of mental health are presented. 59 Ref.

Turner, W. "Alaska Combating Drinking Problem," New York Times. 11, July, 1982. 1p.

The author contends that for years the problem of alcoholism in Alaska, particularly among the State's natives, has been a scandal; however, things may be changing in the 200 or more bush villages where most of the natives live. In this newspaper article, an Alaskan 17 million dollar alcohol program is briefly described, including how villages are given advice on alcoholism, and how the inebriated are jailed in Nome. It is reported that 80 percent of the patients in an expanded treatment center in Nome are from the villages, and there has been a 60 percent drop in calls for the police in 11 villages where liquor has been banned.

United States. Alcohol, Drug Abuse, and Mental Health Administration. Indian in the Red: A Reality or Myth? Rockville, Md., 1977 18 p.

United States. Congress of the U.S. House Committee on Education and Labor. Indian Youth Alcohol and Substance Abuse Prevention Act Committee on Education and Labor Report to Accompany H.R.1156. Washington, D.C: House of Representatives, Ninety-Ninth Congress, Second Sesion, 1986, 26 p.

This document presents a report from the House of Representatives Committee on Education and Labor concerning H.R. 1156, The Indian Youth Alcohol and Substance Abuse Prevention Act. An amended version of the bill, which was proposed to coordinate and expand services for the prevention, identification, treatment, and follow-up care of alcohol and drug abuse among Indian youth, is included. The six titles of the bill are presented as being concerned with 91) inter-departmental agreement and coordination of services (2) education; (3) family and social services: (4) low enforcement; (5) Indian youth alcohol and substance abuse treatment and rehabilitation; and (6) definition of terms. Other sections of the report discuss a summary of the legislation, the legislative history of the bill, and the need for the legislation and provisions of the bill. An explanation of each title of the bill is provided and committee recommendations are given. Oversight, cost estimate, and inflationary impact of the bill are considered and a section-by-section analysis of H.R. 1156 is provided. Finally, changes in existing law made by the bill are reported, specifically changes in the Indian Elementary and Secondary School Assistance Act, the Indian Education Act, the Adult Education Act, and the Education Amendments of 1978. (NB).

United States.   Congress of the U.S. Senate Select
Committee on Indian Affairs.   Indian Juvenile Alcohol
and Drug Abuse Prevention.   Hearing before the Select
Committee on Indian Affairs.   Washington, D.C. United
States Senate, Ninety-Ninth Congress, First Session of
S. 1298 (October 25, 1985, Anchorage, AK., 1986, 71 p.

The Senate Select Committee on Indian Affairs met in
Anchorage Alaska, to hear testimony on a bill (S. 1298)
to coordinate and expand services for the prevention,
identification, and treatment of alcohol and drug abuse
among Indian youth.   Testimony stressed the extent of
alcohol, drug, and other substance abuse among Native
youth in rural Alaska.   Other topics were the need for
coordination between the Bureau of Indian Affairs and
the Indian Health Service, these agencies' lack of
involvement in substance abuse prevention and treatment
programs, and the role of Native health corporations in
substance abuse services.   Representatives of the
Alaska Native community providing testimony included
spokespersons for the Alaska Native Health Board,
Alaska Federation of natives, Copper River Native
Association, Aleutian/Pribilof Islands Association,
Yukon-Kushokwim Health Corporation, Kashunamuit School,
and Tanana Chiefs Council.   Statements by Alaska's
Senator Murkowski and Governor Sheffield are included.

United States.   National Institute on Alcohol Abuse and
Alcoholism "Self-Help Programs for Indians and native
Alaskans," Alcohol Health and Research World 1974 Sum
Exp   Issue 11-16.

Discusses the Efforts of the National Institute on
Alcohol Abuse and Alcoholism (NIAAA) to reduce the high
incidence of alcohol abuse among American Indians and
Alaskan Natives.   Since 1971 almost 100 self-help
programs have been funded to combat alcoholism among
Indians in addition to a mini-grant program making
funds available for Alaskan Natives.   These programs
operate independently, with recipients responsible for
program development, implementation, and expenditure of
funds.   Examples of several treatment facilities
illustrating different approaches to treatment are
presented.   Although most NIAAA funded programs are
short-term, their strength and self-direction will
foster additional support to compat the major social,
health, and economic problems among American Indians.

United States National Institute on Drug Abuse.   Come
Closer Around the Fire: Using Tribal Legends, Myths,
and Stories in Preventing Drug Abuse.   Rockville, Md.,
1980, 32p.

A guide to using tribal stories, myths, and legends as

a tool for preventing the abuse of drugs (including alcohol) among Native Americans is presented. it is intended primarily for people working in the field of drug abuse prevention, but can be used by anyone (teachers, counselors, librarians, elders, parents, community leaders) seeking ways to help Indian young people feel pride in themselves and in their culture.

United States-U.S. Congress, Comptroller General. Comptroller General's Report to the Congress: Congressional Monitoring of Planning for Indian Health Care Facilities is Still Needed. Washington, D.C. 1980, 46 p.

According to this report to congress by the Comptroller General, the Indian Health Service (IHS_, Department of Health, Education and Welfare,has only partially complied with a directive to improve its planning for hospital construction. Although the service revised the way it determines the number of acute care beds needed, GAO believes that planning is still not adequate. One example is the IHS plan to treat alcoholism and mental illness. This plan is the basis for adding 45 acute care beds in the Navajo area. The report states that until IHS can demonstrate that (1) patients needing alcohol detoxification and mental detoxification and psychiatric care would submit to acute care treatment if more beds were available, IHS hospital plans should not add acute care beds to the Navajo area for these services. This document calls for a continuation of the 1977 moratorium imposed by Congress on hospital construction planning by the service until they fully comply with the Congressional directive.

United States. Bureau of Indian Affairs. Results of the Questionnaire on Alcohol and Drug Abuse Survey For Schools Funded Under the Bureau of Indian Affairs: Alcohol and Drug Abuse in BIA Schools. Washington, D. C.,1982.

Findings are summarized from an alcohol and drug abuse questionnaire distributed in May, 1981 to 12 areas and 27 agencies encompassing approximately 224 Bureau of Indian Affairs and Tribal Schools, which serve approximately 44,000 students. General trends and issues concerning alcohol and drug abuse in these schools are discussed, including recommendations for prevention and intervention. A copy of the questionnaire is appended.

United States Indian Health Service, Alcoholism: A High Priority Health Problem, Rockville, MD., 1973, 29 pgs.

Findings of a study of alcohol abuse and alcoholism among American Indians and Alaska Native are reported by the Indian Health Service Task Force On Alcoholism. The incidence of alcoholism among these two groups is estimated to be twice the national average.   The majority of accidents, homicides, assaults, suicides and suicide attempts among Indians are associated with alcohol.   The history, nature, extent, and significance of alcoholism in the Indian population are outlined in orderto provide health personnel with a clearer understanding of this unique problem.   It is noted that it is a particular problem for adult males and adolescents of both sexes. Often due to feelings of anger, frustration, or boredom.   Conflicts between school and home environments create problems for teenagers.   Problems involving prevention, treatment and control of alcoholism are explained, and some components of programs to combat and treat alcoholism are suggested.   These include direct personalservices (general medical care, phychiatric care, counseling programs, detoxification centers, and halfway houses), training programs for those treating Indian alcoholics, health education programs, and community relationships. The final section of the report contains a reference guide to alcoholism programs and resources.

United States. National Institute on Alcohol Abuse and Alcoholism, <u>Seventh Annual Report to the United States Congress: Fiscal Years 1978 and 1979</u>.   Rockville, MD., 1979. 80p.

NIAAA programs and activities during fiscal years 1978 and 1969 are reviewed.   Following a discussion of the background and mission of NIAAA, activities are discussed within the following framework: (1) the development of knowledge about alcoholism through social, psychological, epidemiologic, physiological, and biochemical research, (2) the development of financial and human resources for the treatment of alcoholism, (3) prevention activities, (4) occupational programming activities, and (5) NIAAA founding and evaluation of alcoholism treatment programs. Background information about NIAAA operations, including budgetary information is appended.   Data on youth and American Indian is included here.   11 Ref.

United States National Institute on Drug Abuse. <u>Trainer Manual-Adolescence: Intervention Strategies</u>, by Gillispie, Beth J.; LeClere, Maria; Quaranta, Cathy; Spring, Renee, Rockville, MD., 1979.

This course "was created as a result of a decision to redo the Making a Difference with Youth course developed in 1974.   This decision marked an effort to substantially strengthen the courses pertaining to prevention developed by the National Drug Abuse Center for Training and Resource Development." This course provided the user with an understanding of adolescent development (ages 12-18), and provides knowledge about skills necessary, from an interpersonal standpoint, to deliver quality youth services. It does not include information about specific types of youth programs or about developing a broad agency approach to youth populations.

White, J. C.   "American Indian Youth Alcohol Abuse and Alcoholism Prevention Project".   Dissertation. Dissertation Abstracts International 44 (03z): 878-A, 1983.

The American Indian Center, located in Baltimore, Maryland, was established to alleviate some of the housing, education, medical, and unemployment problems of American Indian population. This prevention project was designed to reduce the stigma of alcoholism and to create a climate where young people would feel free to seek help. The goals of this project included: (1) helping these youth become aware that they are a part of a high-risk population; (2) uncovering the myths of alcohol, alcohol abuse, and alcoholism; (3) creating an awareness of the early warning signs of alcoholism; (4) teaching these youth to teach other youths about alcohol abuse and alcoholism; (5) making youth aware of the resources available in the community; and (6) teaching that alco-holism is a disease, not a moral issue. Results of this project indicate that knowledge can be increased and self worth can change.

Whittaker, J. O.   Alcohol and the Standing Rock Sioux Tribe: A Twenty Year Follow-up Study. Middletown, PA.: Pennsylvania State University, 1980. 38p.

Results of a twenty year follow-up study on the use of alcohol by the Standing Rock Sioux Tribe of the Dakotas are presented and discussed. The author contends that the "symptoms" of alcoholism, derived from studies of white drinkers, present serious problems for cross-cultural research, because many of them may be culturally defined and determined, i. e., they may not be universally characteristic of alcoholism. It has been suggested that behavioral symptoms are less reliable than physiological symptoms because behavioral symptoms are less culture free. The intent of the present investigation (the first long-term longitudinal study of alcohol use by American Indians) was to examine this controversy. An interview schedule was used, which consisted of 118 questions, and divided into the following six parts: (1) pattern of drinking:

(2) motivation for drinking; (3) social control; (4) knowledge about alcohol; (5) results of drinking, and (6) drug and alcohol use.

Many of these questions were used in the original 1960 study, and of these, a number had been employed earlier in a study to provide data on cultural factors which might explain the absence of certain behavioral symptoms of alcoholism typically observed in white alcoholics. From these data, the hypothesis that certain sociocultural variables might exist which mitigate against the appearance of "classic" symptoms of alcoholism was rejected. It is concluded that alcoholism among Indians is more like, than unlike, that observed in non-Indians; that the major difference lies in the incidence of heavy drinking and alcoholism, rather than cultural factors which obscure or mitigate against the presence of certain behavioral symptoms. Recommendations for the prevention of drinking on the reservation are enumerated, and a copy of the confidential drug and alcohol survey questionnaire is appended. 14 Ref.

Zephier, R. L., and Hedin, C. "Alcoholism Among Indian Students: Walking Like You Talk," Conference paper, National Indian Child Conference, Alburquerque, NM: 17-21 May 1981. 16 p.

A number of facts concerning alcohol abuse among native Americans are presented. Alcoholism is shown as the leading cause of death among Indian people, and Native Americans are shown to have a higher alcoholism rate than any minority group in the country. The impact on tribes shows how school age children from kindergarten through the twelfth grade are abusing alcohol to the point that they cannot take advantage of the gains made by the Indian peoples during the 1980s. Lists of suggestions for dealing with student alcohol problems include fundamentals of alcohol education, preparing to deal with the problem drinker, and approaches toward controlling student drinking. Implementation of youth prevention programs is also covered. The need for community involvement is emphasized, and prevention approaches, including provision of support to existing alcoholism programs, implementation of prevention activities in schools, and development of a community based prevention project are presented.

7

RESERVATIONS

Beauvais, Fred; Oetting, E.R.; Edwards, R.W. "Trends in Drug Use of Indian Adolescents Living on Reservations: 1975-1983," American Journal of Drug Use and Alcohol Abuse. 1985. vol 11(3-4). 209-229.

Buehlmann, J. "Which Way The Morrow," Rockville, MD.: NCALI, 1976, 41 p.

A report on alcoholism and alcohol abuse on the Yankton Sioux reservation from 1 Oct 1975 to 31 Mar 1976 is presented. Initially the project was aimed at hardcore alcohol abusers, but was later altered to include youth in the areas of education and prevention. Statistics covering clinical visits and hospital admissions were related to alcoholism and alcohol abuse in 48-55 percent of the figures. It was found that at least 97 percent of all arrests during one 20-month period were alcohol related. Areas of prevention and treatment viewed by the author as essential to an overall comprehensive program are discussed.

Cockerham, William "Drinking Attitudes And Practices Among Wind River Reservation Indian Youth," Journal of Studies on Alcohol 36(3): 321-326, 1975.

The attitudes toward drinking of a cohort of 7th and 8th grade American Indian students, mostly Arapahoe and Shoshone living on Wyoming's Wind River Reservation, were studied. Data were collected by means of a survey questionnaire administered to 144 Indian students attending the three junior high schools on the Wind River Reservation. Despite the possibility of getting into trouble for illegal drinking, the students stated positive attitudes toward drinking. This finding was common among both boys and girls. Although boys began drinking at an earlier age than girls, most of these Indian youths said they had begun a pattern of regular drinking by the age of 13. It is concluded that attitudes toward drinking among Wind River Indian youth, both on an individual and peer-group basis, are supported by a norm of approval or at least a strong tolerance of drinking. 10 Ref.

Delk, John L. et al. "Drop-outs from an American Indian Reservation School: A Possible Prevention Program," Journal of Community Psychology. 1974 Jan., vol 2(1) 15-17.

Home patterns as a primary factor in the backgrounds of dropouts. Lack of parent control was found in five of seven dropouts; four of five had a history of arrests for intoxication; three females had children born out of wedlock two were married; two had delinquent siblings; and one had an alcoholic father. None of these factors was present in any of the controls. School data that best discriminated between the samples were those of truancy, mild mental retardation, desire to leave school, aggressive behavior, and withdrawal from peers. Again, none of these factors underlying dropping-out were present in controls. It was concluded that the two primary factors underlying dropping-out were lack of parent control and mental retardation, and a correction program was undertaken employing special education. Preliminary data after one year indicate a decline in delinquent behaviors and no new dropouts.

Forslund, Morris A. Drug Use and Delinquency. Data Book 3, Laramie, Wyoming: Governor's Planning Committee on Criminal Administration, 1974, 49 pgs.

The nature and magnitude of the drug use and delinquency problem among youth living in Wyoming's Wind River Indian Reservation area were investigated in May 1972. A drug user was defined as any student who used marijuana or any other drug for pleasure or kicks during the preceding year. A self-report questionnaire was administered to 456 male and 391 female students at Lander Valley High School and Wind River High School. Some findings were: (1) 79.8 percent of the males and 81.1 percent of the females had used neither marijuana nor other drugs during the past year; (2) 1.1 percent of the males and 2.3 percent of the females had used other drugs but not marijuana; (3) 12.5 percent of the males and 7.7 percent of the females had used marijuana but not other drugs; and (4) 6.6 percent of the males and 9.0 percent of the females had used both marijuana and other drugs. This data book consists of 87 tables of data giving the responses to questionnaire items by drug and sex. Levels of significance are indicated below the tables when the differences existing in

the response distribution have a probability of less
that 5 in 100 of being attributable to chance. (SHB)

Pemberton, Alfred R.: Harper, Dennis   Alternative
Approach to Reservation Youth Problems. Cass Lake,
Minnesota: Leech Lake Reservation Youth Center, 1974,
32 p. NTIS PB-270 403/9SL.

In this research and demonstration grant project, the
Leech Lake Indian Reservation Youth Center (LLRYC) used
alternative, rather than traditional, social work
methods to help reservation based Native American Youth
meet problems of education, drug and alcohol abuse, and
juvenile delinquency. About 300 youths participated in
LLRYC activities which proved effective in increasing
school attendance and completion, and in combating
alcohol and drug abuse and juvenile delinquency.
Native American staff were best able to develop empathy
and trust with Indian youth.

Pinto, Leonard J. "Alcohol and Drug Abuse Among Native
American Youth on Reservations: A Growing Crisis,"
Vol. 1: Appendix, In Drug Use In America: Problem in
Perspective, Washington, D. C.,: Government Printing
Office, 1973 1157-1178. (SUDOCS # Y 3 M33/2:1/973).

The author reviews research on drinking and other drug
abuse among American Indian Youth, in relation to low
educational achievement, poor health, and high rate of
unemployment and delinquency; the relationship of
social scientific thinking to Indian Reservation life,
the cultural, psychological, and sociopolitical factors
which account for the repeated failure of American
society, particularly the Federal Government, to
respect Native American rights and aid them in
achieving independence. Suggestions include turning
over control of the educational system to the Indian
groups who want it, continuation of alcohol and suicide
prevention programs, and the reinstitution of the
civilian conservation corps. 50 Ref.

Pooley, Albert M., Miller, Dorothy "Patterns of
Substance Abuse Among Navajo Public School Students,"
Fort Defiance, Arizona: Indian Health Service, 1979,
(42 pgs.).

This study examines the prevalence of alcohol and drug
abuse among a sample of 504 8th, 9th, and 11th graders
attending five public schools on the Navajo
reservation. Health, education, social service and
substance abuse workers and law enforcement officials
were also interviewed concerning their evaluation of
the type and extent of the problem. A discussion of

findings includes agency workers' general perceptions, agency workers' recommendations, students' responses on types of users, prevalence of substance abusers, and social factors of substance abusers. The report concludes with a summary of findings and recommendations for solutions to the problem of alcohol and drug abuse.

Topper, M. D. "Drinking as an Expression of Status: Navajo Male Adolescents," Drinking Behavior Among Southwestern Indians, Tucson, AZ: University of Arizona Press, 1980, 248 p. (pp. 103-147).

A methodology for the study of drinking behaviors, which views the phenomenon of drinking on three levels (cultural, social, and individual), is presented. This methodology combines the elicitation techniques of cognitive anthropology with a functional analysis of what drinking does to help bolster the individual and the culture in the struggle for survival. Adolescent drinking, "problem drinking," and some proposed causes of "Navajo alcoholism" are discussed. Because many Navajos who drink do not drink like Anglo-Americans, some of the theoretical issues that have been raised about the nature of the phenomenon of drinking and its proper ethnographic description are addressed. 17 Ref.

Tyler, John D.; Cohen, Keith N.; Clark, Janet S. "Providing Community Consultation in a Reservation Setting," Journal of Rural Community Psychology, 3; 1, 1982

The purpose of this project was to devise a program of culturally appropriate psychological services for 2,000 Sioux Indians on a North Dakota reservation. Particular focus was paid to unique problems of these Indians including alcoholism, suicide, and depression. Also of relevance to the program was incorporation of Sioux' customs and values in dealing with individual clients, and promoting effective interactions with native paraprofessional consultees. A youth council was established and community education was promoted. For purposes of this program, the reservation is considered a semiclosed system for administering human services.

Weast, Donald E. "Patterns of Drinking Among Indian Youth: The Significance of Anomia and Differential Association," The Wisconsin Socialist. 1972, 9, 1, Win, 12-28.

The history of problems connected with alcohol drinking among American Indian is reviewed. Despite a voluminous literature, there is little definitive evidence of the extent of alcohol consumption among Indians and how it relates to specific social-psychological factors. Research among the Oneida Indians on a reservation (population about 1,600) about 6 miles from Green Bay, Northeastern Wisc., is reported which documents on how Indian youths learn patterns of heavy drinking. Data were obtained from a questionnaire administered to 90 Oneida Indian teenagers attending one of these high schools. It was hypothesized that those youths with a high degree of anomia will be likely to adopt a heavy drinking "way of life," A modified version of Srole's Anomia Scale was used. Four levels of anomia were discerned in the collected data. A chi square test revealed a statistically significant and positive relationship between anomia and alcohol consumption of the Indians but not among the whites. However, the percent of heavy drinkers decreases from 72.7% in the high anomia category to 65% in the very high anomia category. Further analysis of the data taking into account contact with heavy drinking patterns, changes the lack of correlation between anomia and alcohol consumption to a strong inverse relationship. The evidence indicates that there are approximately equal numbers of abstainers, light drinkers, moderate and heavy drinkers among the Oneidas. This distribution is quite similar to that for the white control group. Indian youth were found to exhibit extreme diversity in their drinking patterns. Future research should assume heterogeneity rather than a similarity in the biographies of individual Indians to discover those factors which account for the variability.

8

SOCIOLOGICAL FACTORS

Adams, Doris (et al.) <u>Report of the Michigan Interim Action Committee On Indian Problems</u> Lansing, Michigan: Michigan State Interim Action Committee on Indian Problems. 1971, 40 p.

Stressing the importance of American Indian involvement in affairs affecting Michigan's Indian population, this report by the Interim Action Committee on Indian problems presents recommendations relative to education, employment, health, and the commission on Indian Affairs. Recommendations for the commission emphasize: Leadership at the local, state and federal levels; educational program development; welfare eligibility information; legal education; budgetary responsibilities; Priority programming; on-going evaluations; etc. Health recommendations focus on remedial actions pertinent to: Infant mortality rates, adult death rates, malnutrition, alcoholism the training of professional Indian health workers, etc. Employment recommendations call for: In service training of Michigan concentrated employment programs (MCEP) Staff, revision of the Bureau of Indian Affairs' relocation procedures, coordination between program development and the inter tribal councils of Michigan, etc. Economic development recommendations focus on land use and industrial development and skill training in specific nonreservation areas. Educational recommendations call for a needs assessment, an Indian education staff in the Department of Education and an Indian Education Committee to advise the State Board of Education, a 5-year reading literacy goal, etc.

Adams, Gerald H. <u>American Indians. Volume I.</u> 1964-1975. NTIS/PS-77/0894/4SL, 1977, 170 p.

Volume I and a two volume documentation of the social and economic characteristics of American Indians begins citations on age groups, on and off reservation populations, employment, income, education, alcoholism, crime, Social Welfare, Family relations, community development, natural resource management, historical areas, housing, health, land use, industrial affairs, training, and other aspects of a minority group. Tribal affairs and federal programs are included.

Allison, MacBurnie Education and the Mesquakie.   Ph.D. Dissertation. Iowa State University. 1974.

The purpose of the study was to record a picture of the major forces which have affected Mesquakie education. The study concerns conditions and events which took place over the last century.   The study may serve as a model for further investigations of educational background for other specific geographic and ethnic groups.   Obtaining the material for this study entailed wide reading of written sources, trips to Indian boarding school at Flandreau, South Dakota, and Lawrence, Kansas, and interviews with many persons concerned with Mesquakie education.   Interviews included Mesquakie tribal members, Bureau of Indian Affairs personnel, boarding school teachers, and the current missionary serving the Mesquakie United Presbyterian Church.   The Mesquakie have experienced most of the negative aspect associated historically with Indian education and life.   The regimentation of the boarding schools, government day school education (which did not begin for the Mesquakie on a major scale until 1930), have all been a part of the tribe's experience.   Efforts to make farmers of the reluctant Mesquakie did not end until 1950.   Alcoholism has been a problem for two centuries.   Poverty continues into the seventies.   The main religion of the tribe is the Native Bundle religion despite proselyting by Presbyterians, Mormons, Assembly of God members, and the building of a white log church by the Church of the Nazarene.   The basic language of the tribe remains Mesquakie -- a language shared with several other tribes including the Sac and the Pottawatomie.   Court cases over treaties with the government, court cases about law and order on the settlement and court cases concerning school conditions have all failed to give the Mesquakie a clear direction to follow in education. Mesquakie education remains a difficult and occasionally bitter problem despite continual efforts of numerous individuals to blend the Mesquakie education into the public schools.

Alu Like Inc.   A Report on Mental Health and Substance Abuse Among the Native Hawaiian Population, Honolulu, Hawaii: Alu Like, Inc., 1979.

The purpose of this study is to clearly identify those segments of the Native Hawaiian population who are most in need of services and to gather data for more successful program planning. Data on participants in federally-funded mental health and substance abuse programs who are Native Hawaiian were collected, computerized, and analyzed. Findings can be summarized as follows: the Native Hawaiian family is still a strong, functioning unit. In light of the sometimes overwhelming stresses placed upon them in a bicultural setting, the extended family most often than not provides the needed support for recovery. Thus, the major focus for a mental health program for the Native Hawaiian population has to be to help strengthen the family and, in those cases where the family has disintegrated beyond repair, to provide the disturbed individual with a substitute family situation. The three areas where such a program is needed most are in alcoholism, family violence, and teenage problems such as suicide and drug abuse.

Andre, James, M. American Indian Drinking Patterns. Rockville, Md.: Indian Health Service, 1979, 24 p.

The purpose of this paper was to present information concerning drinking patterns of Native American Indians. The study is divided into five parts and includes discussions of such topics as historical background, changes in U.S. patterns of alcohol consumption, American Indian drinking patterns, and "Firewater myths." Results of the study also include explanations of Indian drinking patterns. These include poor role models for drinking behavior, effects of Indian wars, confinement to reservations, growing affluence, poverty, lack of cultural experience with alcohol, introduction of alcohol too early in childhood, expectations, deculturation, to escape, and other such explanations. DAR.

Andre, James M. "Alcohol Abuse and the American Indian: A Report on the Impact," Department of the Interior and Related Agencies Appropriations for 1980. Part 8.

This study presents the impact of alcohol abuse on American Indians in two categories: Mortality and Morbidity. Results show that in the overall data for all areas and tribes served by the Indian Health Service, five of the top ten causes of death among Indian people are directly related to alcohol abuse. Also approximately 70 percent of all treatment services provided by the IHS are for alcohol-related conditions. KEW.

Attneave, Carolyn L.: Beiser, Morton. Service Networks
and Patterns of Utilization: Mental Health Programs,
Indian Health Service (IHS) Volume I: Overview and
Recommendations. Rockville, Md.: Indian Health
Service, 1975, 190 p.

Constituting an overview of a ten volume report on the
historical development and contemporary activities
(1966-1973) of each of the eight administrative area
offices of the Indian Health Service (IHS) mental
health programs, this volume includes: The methods
used for data collection (personal interviews with both
past and present IHS key officials, area site visits,
and examination of area reports); The report's
limitations; the historical context for viewing the
introduction of mental health programs into IHS; the
headquarters for mental health programs located in
Albuquerque, New Mexico; the major accomplishments of
IHS Mental health programs; selected themes appearing
in the area narratives (often in terms of polarities of
opinion and practice); and seventy-six specific
recommendations for identified problem areas.
Recommendations discuss issues yet to be resolved which
include: Need for epidemiologic data; adoption and
integration of mental health services with indigenous
cultures and practices; balance between direct and
indirect mental health services; mental health
consultation activities with other IHS staff and
external agencies; services for special populations;
alcoholism and alcohol abuse; drug abuse and inhalants;
accidents, violence; and suicide; and issues internal
to IHS and mental health program administration
(evaluation: recruitment, selection and retention of
professional and paraprofessional personnel;
institutional racism; etc.).

Attneave, Carolyn L., Beiser, Morton. Service Networks
and Patterns of Utilization: Mental Health Programs,
Indian Health Service (IHS), Volume3: Alaska
(Anchorage) Area, 1966-1973. Rockville, Maryland,
Indian Health Service; 1975, 136 p.

The third volume in a ten volume report on the
historical development (1966-1973) of the eight
administrative area offices of the Indian Health
Service (IHS) Mental health programs, this report
presents information on the Alaska area office.
Included in this document are: (1) The context
(geography and demography of Alaska, IHS and regional
relationships with other agencies); (2) The initial
stage: Introduction of IHS Mental Health Services (the
original mental health unit and the concept of patients
as people); (3) Growth: Development of specialized
services (whether to be a special medical ward,

psychological school consultations, alcoholism programs, and training with police and state troopers); (4) Expansions: Development 1968-1973 (budget and personnel changes, dividing responsibility with the state department of mental health, and reciprocity through consultation); (5) Decentralization (Nome, 1971-1972 IHS mental health activities, Anchorage's Alaska Native Medical Center, other service units, and summary); (6) Patient characteristics and flow; (7) An overview (current and potential problems--urban emphasis, staff morale, paraprofessional utilization, budget, need for epidemiology, administrative clarity, etc., and achievement--balanced development, personnel retention, relationships with other agencies, patient involvement, developmental tasks and evaluation; (8) Appendix.

Attneave, Caroyln L., Reiser, Morton. Service Networks and Patterns of Utilization: Mental Health Programs, Indian Health Services (IHS). Volume4: Albuquerque Area, 1966-1973. Rockville, Md.: Indian Health Service, 1975, 111 p.

The fourth volume in a ten volume report on the historical development (1966-1973) of the eight administrative area offices of the Indian Health Service (IHS) mental health programs, this report presents information on the Albuquerque area office. Included in this report are: (1) The context (geographic distribution; IHS facilities; population served; and culture of the American Indians served--Pueblo, Ute, Jicarilla Apache, and Mescalero Apache); (2) Introduction of mental health services (personnel for 1967, 1968, and 1969 summer); (3) Expansion and development of mental health programs (continuation of northern sections; tensions between two psychiatrists, administration from 1970 to present, hiring mental health coordinators from 1970 to present,1971 clinical psychologist and development of Sr. Catherine's school project and other activities at Laguna and Acoma); (4) Rounding out program development (contract care in a mental health program with emphasis on inpatient and alcoholism services and the children's program, 1972 to present staff completion, special interest in alcoholism program developments, and current Jemez and Mescalero developments); (5) General observations (description of staff consultation activities, 1974 change of command, problems, and accomplishments).

Attneave, Caroyln L, Reiser, Morton. Service Networks and Patterns of Utilization: Mental Health Programs, Indian Health Service (IHS), Volume 5: Billings Area, 1963-1973. Rockville, Md.: Indian Health Service, 1975, 243 p.

As the fifth volume in a ten volume report on the
historical development (1966-1973) of the eight
administrative area offices of the Indian Health
Service (IHS) Mental Health Programs, this report
presents information on the Billings area office.
Included in this document are: (1) General description
(geography, demography, and transportation facilities
and problems); (2) social service branch sponsorship
prior to 1969 (development of consultation contracts
1963-1968, report prepared for budget hearings December
1968, and outline for mental health career development
fellowship hearings December 1968); (3) Continuity:
First chief of Billings' mental health programs
(expanding the role learned as a resident, expansion of
service unit staffing, serving as an IHS consultant);
(4) Discontinuity: Second chief of mental health
programs (two chiefs at once, a new model of service
standards, status and power struggles mirrored in the
service units, and educational network developed; (5)
current status of service unit programs: 1973 (program
descriptions of: Blackfeet, Flathead, Rocky Boy's,
Fort Belknap, Fort Peck, Crow, Northern Cheyenne, and
Wind River Reservations; Intermountain school; and
detoxification programs); (6) Efforts to restore
stability.

Attneave, Carolyn l., Beiser, Morton. Service Networks
and Patterns of Utilization: Mental Health Programs,
Indian Health Service (IHS), Volume 9: Portland Area,
1966-1973. Rockville, Md.: Indian Health Service,
1975, 185 p.

The ninth volume in a ten volume report on the
historical development (1966 - 1973) of the eight
administrative area offices of the Indian Health
Service (IHS) mental health programs, this report
presents information on the Portland area office.
Included in this document are: (1) The context (early
history of the Oregon Territory, geography and tribal
characteristics, population of American Indians served
by IHS, and the area office and transportation links);
(2) Mental Health activities prior to 1969 (University
of Washington Medical School at Yakima and Neah Bay and
Fort Hall suicide prevention program); (3) First full
time mental health team in 1969 (staff, consultation
patterns; objectives; and special projects such as
foster homes, peptic ulcer study of Makah tribe,
alcohol abuse treatment planning, etc.); (4) 1970 -
1972 program development (staff and special
programs/projects including Chemawa boarding school,
Warm Springs mental health and alcohol project, etc.);
(5) 1973 - 1974 program developments (staffing
patterns; staff activity; selected service unit
programs including Northwest Coastal tribes, Rocky

Mountain tribes, Great Basin reservations, and Columbia plateau reservations); (6) Warm Springs: Health program (Warm Springs reservation, alcohol abuse program, children's group home, multiple problem family project, major mental illness, coordination of total program success characteristics,

Attneave, Carolyn L., Ed.: Kelso, Dianne R., Ed. American Indian Annotated Bibliography of Mental Health, Volume . Rockville, Md., Washington Univ., Seattle, National Inst. of Mental Health, 1977. 436 pgs.

Presenting 250 abstracted entries and an additional 250 citations, this bibliography on American Indian mental health is derived form: personal collections; other bibliographies; dissertations; government documents; and five computerized bibliographic data banks. Included in this document are (1) a user's guide to the bibliography; (2) a tribe and culture area index; (3) a subject index (d scriptors with individual definitions); (4) an author index; and (5) an appendix which provides categorical listings of the descriptors used to index each citation.   Each of the annotated citations includes: an author, title, date (the span is approximately 1940 through 1976 publications), publisher, identifier(s) (uncontrolled indexing terms such as tribal names); descriptors (controlled indexing terms); an abstract; and a section called "comments" (e.g., "The anthropological tone of the article which uses unfortunate terms such as 'primitive' and 'pre-scientific,' hurts the article whose attitude toward Navajo culture and traditional healing is basically positive.")   The indexing vocabulary of 277 descriptors is grouped into the following 15 categories: mental health research; environment; population groups and developmental groups; mental health systems; medical system; social work system; education system; religious system (non-Native); legal-correctional system; governmental system; program management and delivery of services; mental health problems and/or concerns; Native American coping mechanisms, norms, values, and cultural resources; Native American culture areas; and Native American Tribes.   This was later revised and published as a book by Greenwood Press, in 1981.

Attneave, C. "American Indians and Alaska Native Families: Emigrants in Their Own Homeland," In M. McGoldrick, et al., Eds., Ethnicity and Family Therapy. New York, NY: Guilford Press, 1982.   600 p. (pp.53-83).

The author describes some of the demographic characteristics of American Indians and Alaska Natives,

some of the problems these populations encounter and
their relationship to family therapists. Ways in which
the general middle class in the United States and the
American Indian and Alaska Native cultures prioritize
their manner of dealing with five basic problems of
relations are discussed. These topic areas of
relationship include: (1) man to nature, or
environment; (2) time orientation; (3) relations with
people; (4) mode of activity idealized; and (5) nature
of man. The association between alcoholism and
suicide, and the fetal alcohol syndrome among American
Indians are also discussed, including strengths of
Indian families. 27 Ref.

Attneave, C. L., Beiser, M. "Mental Disorders Among
Native American Children: Rates and Risk Periods for
Entering Treatment," American Journal of Psychiatry,
139 (2): 193-198, 1982.

National data on the use of outpatient mental health
services by Native American children in 1974 are
compared with 1969 national data on non-Indian
children. It was found that, at all ages except five
to nine years, Indian children were at higher risk for
entering the treatment system than were non-Indian
children, and that utilization patterns varied by age
and sex. Alcohol misuse as an antisocial behavior
problem among Indian teenagers between 15 and 19 years
old was evident. Possible reasons for these high risk
rates demonstrated by Indian children are discussed,
including implications for further studies. 30 Ref.

Bane, William; Goodluck, Charlotte American Indian
Youth Resource Guide, Washington, D. C. : Children's
Bureau (DHHS/ OHS), 1984, ERIC ED 249024.

This was published by the family resource center, a
federally funded project designed to develop and share
resources and information on youth services, child
abuse and neglect, and child welfare in Region VIII,
which includes Colorado, Utah, Wyoming, North Dakota,
South Dakota, and Montana. This resource guide
contains introductory statistical information on the
Indian population and state foster care of Indian
children in this region. The major part of the Guide
lists resources pertaining to services for American
Indian youth. The listings in the resource guide
pertain to various topic areas, such as strengthening
Indian families and youth, strengthening Indian
identity, youth participation and development, teen
parenting among Indian youth, youth abuse and neglect
among American Indians, drug abuse and Indian youth,
delinquency and status offenders, runaways, residential
treatment facilities, independent living programs and

emancipation services, and suicide among Indian youth. Each listing contains names and addresses of national resources, specific Indian programs, contacts in and out of the region, ideas for funding sources, and a bibliography. Six selected youth programs in Region VIII that serve Indian youth are described in the last section of the guide.

Barnes, G.M.; Welte, J.W. "Patterns and Predictors of Alcohol Use Among 7-12th Grade Students in New York State," Journal of Studies on Alcohol 1986, Jan. 47(1). p.53-62.

A survey was conducted to determine prevalence and patterns in the use of alcohol and other substances among 7-12th grade students in New York State. Of this representative sample of 27,335 secondary school students, 71 percent are drinkers and 13 percent are heavy drinkers, i.e., they drink at least once a week and typically consume 5 or more drinks per occasion. White and American Indian students have higher rates of drinking and of heavy drinking than do Hispanic, black, West Indian and Oriental students. The rates of drinking in New York state are higher than those reported in recent national surveys of adolescents. The heavy drinking student can be characterized by frequent school misconduct, first becoming drunk at an early age, having a greater number of friends who get drunk weekly, parental approval of drinking, poor grades in school, being an older adolescent, and being male and white. Author-abstract.

Beauvais, F., Oetting, E. R. " Drug Acquisition Curve: A Method for the Analysis and Prediction of Drug Epidemiology," International Journal of the Addictions 18 (8): 1115-1129, 1983.

A method is presented for charting how a group might acquire exposure to a drug, with the resulting drug acquisition curve having a number of different parameters that describe the group's drug involvement. These key parameters include: (1) the age of exposure when the group begins to use the drug in greater numbers, probably because of exposure to drug-using peers; (2) the acquisition rate, the percent of the group who are newly exposed each year (a rate that is surprisingly constant over as much as five years); and (3) the asymptote, establishing the total percent of the group who will eventually try the drug. Data from the application of acquisition curves for sequential age cohorts are provided, indicating the changing trends in these parameters and their use in predicting future drug prediction of drug epidemiology among a cohort of American Indian children proved to be quite accurate for alcohol and inhalants, but not for marijuana. It is concluded that this method shows considerable potential for documenting drug exposure, for analyzing its occurrence in groups, and for prediction; however, more work is needed to establish the validity of factors that underlie or determine different parameters of the acquisition curve.   6 Ref.

Binion, Jr., Arnold; Miller, C. Dean; Beauvais, Fredrick; Oetting, Eugene R.   "Rationales for the use of Alcohol, Marijuana, and Other Drugs by Eighth-Grade Native American and Anglo Youth," The International Journal of the Addictions, 23(1) January, 1988, pp, 47-64.

This study examined rationales for alcohol, marijuana, and other drug use among Indian and non-Indian youth. Differences were found between reservation Indian and rural non-Indian rationales for alcohol, marijuana and other drug use. A majority of both Indian and non-Indian eighth graders indicate that they use drugs to enhance positive affective states, for excitement, for parties, to be with friends, to relax, and to handle negative affective states including worries and nervousness. Indian youth appear to also use drugs to cope with boredom. Unlike non-Indian youth, Indian youth have no strong rationale for their use of other drugs. Interventions will have to be impactful and pervasive in order to counter the many positive and negative rationales associated with drug use.

Broudy, David W.; May, Phillip A.   "Demographic and Epidemiologic Transition Among the Navajo Indians," Social Biology 1983, Spr. vol. 30(1)   1-16.

Analyzed mortality and natality data for Navajos compiled by the Indian Health Service. It is contended that the major implications for social and health planning with the Navajos result from the social change toward modernization.   Their higher-than-average mortality rate reflects deaths from vehicle accidents, alcoholism, suicide, homicide, and cirrhosis of the liver.   In addition to public awareness and emergency medical services, culturally sensitive economic development must be encouraged.   Demographic and epidemiologic transitions are underway among Navajo Indians.   (29 Ref.).

Canadian Journal of Public Health.   "Health of Native Canadians: Its Relevance to World Health,"   73(5): 297-298, 1982.

In this editorial, the health problems of Native Canadians are discussed as they relate to world health, and how a solution to these problems may be found in other countries. It is contended that the worst of the problems of Native Canadians, not so often encountered in developing nations, is the consequences of alcohol and other substance abuse. In early adult life it is all too easy to submit to the temptation to escape the harsh reality of life in a shattered society by impairing the senses with alcohol. 2 Ref.

Chafetz, M., Ed. Research on Alcoholism: Clinical Problems and Special Populations Journal Citation Proceedings: 1st Annual Alcoholism Conference of NIAAA, Rockville, Md.: National Institute on Alcohol Abuse and Alcoholism, 1971, 377 p.

This book is a compilation of the conference papers delivered at the first annual alcoholism conference of NIAAA. The topics chosen reflect NIAAA's research priorities. The conference is divided into two general subject areas, clinical problems and alcohol problems in special population groups. Clinical problems are subdivided into medical complications of alcoholic persons, pharmacological considerations, and behavioral techniques. Population groups are subdivided into American Indians, youth, drinking drivers, and alcoholic women.

Chen, Martin K., Berg, Lawrence E., London, Virginia. The Health of Native Americans in Alaska: An Exploratory Study. Hyattsville, Maryland: National Center for Health Services Research, 1977, 22 p.

This study focuses attention on three selected health problems that are believed by Indian Health Service officials to be prevalent among Native Americans in Alaska: Alcoholism, heart disease and pneumonia/influenza. By means of an index specifically designed for assessing the health status of disadvantaged minority populations, it was found that the Native Americans fared better in heart disease, but were worse off in alcoholism and pneumonia/influenza. It was further found that the rankings of the index values for the four ethnic groups in Alaska -- the Aleuts, the Athabascans, The Eskimos and the Tlinket-Haidans -- were negatively related to the subjective evaluations of their relative health status by thirteen health workers intimately involved in providing care to the natives. Alternative explanations for this phenomenon were offered.

Cohen, S. "Alcohol and the Indian," Drug Abuse and Alcoholism Newsletter 11(4): 1-3, 1982

It is stated that alcoholism among Indians is more than

two and maybe as much as four times the national level and is higher than for any other minority. The first ten causes of death among Indians include five that are directly or indirectly due to alcohol abuse. These are alcohol related accidents, cirrhosis, alcoholism, suicide, and homicide. The are biochemical and metabolic factors (e.g., Oriental flush syndrome, ineffective metabolism of ethanol), as well as cultural, social and familial ones which affect the high rate of alcoholism among Indians. Drinking patterns among Indians are not monolithic, but there are some patterns that are more characteristic of Indians than of other groups. It is argued that the present policy of placing few family and social sanctions on the young person's drinking, the excessive drinking role models provided by older relatives, and the symbolic rewards from drunkenness all contribute to perpetuate destructive drinking practices. An entire generation of children will have to be educated about the self-destructive and genocidal nature of current alcohol consumption styles and provided with alternative forms of socializing, Otherwise, the process will continue and a third of the Indian population will succumb to the multiple lethalities of this single drug.

Cockerham, William C.; Forslund, Morris A., Roboin, Rolland M. "Drug Use Among White and American Indian Indian High School Students," International Journal of the Addictions, 11, 1976, pp. 209-220.

The authors administered a questionnaire to 391 white and 120 American Indian 9th-12th graders to ascertain the nature and extent of drug use. Data indicate that Indian subjects had a more favorable attitude toward the use of marijuana and other drugs than did white subjects. Indian subjects were also more likely than white subjects to try using marijuana and other drugs, but no more likely than Whites to continue using such drugs after having tried them.

Colley, Carol "Student Perceptions of the Chemawa Alcohol Education Center," Masters Thesis, 1973, 64 pgs.

This study investigated student perceptions of the alcohol education center at the Chemawa Indian School. The paper forwards a review of literature on adolescent drinking with special care taken to provide information concerning drinking done by Indian youth. Methodology used to examine student perceptions involved a series of interviews conducted with each individual who entered the Alcohol Education Center during a one week period. Demographic data, information on patterns of

participation and student ideas were ascertained
through the interviewing technique. Conclusions drawn
by the author include: 1) the current program was
preferred over the previous year's by students
interviewed, 2) those students brought in for drinking
violations were more involved in counseling; 3) the
students interviewed had a need for the alcohol center.
Findings were inconclusive regarding student ideas for
needed change, the most important means of advertising
was counselor outreach, and that participation
differences existed between Northwest and Alaskan
students.

DArcy, C. Bold, G. "Alcohol and Drug Dependency in
Saskatchewa, 1969-1974," Journal of Studies on
Alcohol. 1983, July. 44(4). p 630-46.

The demographic characteristics and the trends in
health care utilization of alcohol and drug dependent
residents of the Canadian province of Saskatchewan from
1969 to 1974 are examined. Author.

Everett, Michael, W.; Waddell, Jack O.; Heath, Dwight
B. Cross Cultural Approaches to the Study of Alcohol:
An Interdisciplinary Perspective. Conference on
Alcohol Studies and Anthropology, Chicago, Ill.:
Aldine Publ., 1976, 432 p.

This volume is a product of the conference on alcohol
studies and anthropology which was jointly organized by
editors. The conference was funded by the National
Institute on Alcohol Abuse and Alcoholism, NIMH and
sponsored by the Smithsonian Institution's Center for
the Study of Man. The conference was held at the
University of Chicago, August 28-30, 1973 as part of
the IXth International Congress of Anthropological and
Ethnological Sciences. This volume brings together
some of the keynote papers that were presented at the
conference to stimulate discussion. Individual papers
were incorporated for their evaluative merit and
descriptive content. The volume emphasizes: (1)
variety of ways that drinking behavior can be observed,
described, analyzed and interpreted; (2) what the cross
cultural perspective of anthropology has contributed to
alcohol studies; and (3) what alcohol studies conducted
in other disciplines have contributed to this cross-
cultural perspective on alcoholism.

Ferguson, Frances N. "Similarities and Differences
Among A Heavily, Arrested Group of Navajo Indian
Drinkers in a Southwestern American Town," In Cross-
Cultural Approaches to The Study of Alcohol. ed. by M.
W. Everett; J. O. Waddell; D. B. Heath, Paris, France,
Mouton, 1976, pp 161-171.

Some common attributes of public drinking among Navajos are discussed, and the results of a study of 110 frequently arrested Navajo men are presented. The public (outdoor) nature of drinking among this group is well documented; however, a stereotype or casual profile of a Navajo man with multiple alcohol-associated arrests would not reveal the variety of types. Substantial intragroup differences were found in age, education, kind of employment, and, by implication, degree of acculturation. This group of men included persons accustomed to modern employment and persons who were self-employed in traditional occupations, college graduates and illiterates, professionals and laborers, residents of town and country, and elders and youths. It is concluded that a common drinking style has masked differences greater than the similarities.

Forslund, M.A. "Functions of Drinking for Native American and White Youth," Journal of Youth and Adolescence; 7, 1978, pp. 327-332.

Few studies have dealt with the functions of drinking for Native American and white youth. The findings presented here are based on responses to a self-report questionnaire administered to 9th through 12th-grade students at two high schools in Fremont County, Wyoming--the county where the great majority of Wyoming's Native American population resides. Based on work by Jessor, Carman and Grossman, 30 items concerning positive-social, personal-effect, and experiential reasons for drinking were examined. Although there are some statistically significant differences in responses to individual items and statistically significant differences between Indian and white males and females on the personal-effect and positive-social categories of items, the functions of drinking appear to be quite similar for these Indian and white youth.

Gregory, Dick "Racial Differences in the Incidence and prevalence of Alcohol Abuse in Oklahoma," Alcohol Technical Reports, 4(4): 37-44, 1975.

Data are presented on the prevalence and incidence of alcoholism among blacks, Indians, and whites in Oklahoma. American Indians, male and female, were found to have the highest rates of alcohol abuse. Blacks were found to have the lowest male and female alcohol arrest rate in the juvenile population, but the second highest rate in the adult population. Sixty-nine percent of alcoholic Indians were incorporated in the treatment delivery system as compared with 18 percent of black and 19 percent of white alcohol abusers. 7 Ref.

Goldstein, G. S.; Oetting, E. R.; Edwards, R; et. al. "Drug Abuse Among Native American Young Adults," International Journal of the Addictions 14: 855-860, 1979.

Drug use was surveyed among 276 Native American (i.e., Indian) students (aged 18-27; 149 women) of a postsecondary educational institution (the institution is located in an urban environment and provides training in arts and technical skills for talented youth from Indian reservations). The use of all drugs was much higher than in other samples of college age youth; beer, distilled spirits, and marijuana were the most popular drugs; 41, 20, 27 and 6 percent of the sample considered themselves moderate to heavy users of beer, distilled spirits, marijuana, and amphetamine, respectively; 20 percent used amphetamines in the past 2 months and 21 percent had tried inhalants though there was little present use. Ten percent were involved in the drug subculture, using multiple drugs relatively heavily.

Green, B. E.: Sack, W. H.; Pambrum, A. "Review of Child Psychiatric Epidemiology with Special Reference to American Indian and Alaska Native Children," White Cloud Journal American Indian Mental Health, 2 (No.2): 22z--36, 1981.

The prevalence of alcohol use among American Indian children and in the majority culture populations is discussed in a review of child psychiatric epidemiology. Child alcohol use may have risen over the past decade: a 1972 study of 5050 students reported 59 percent alcohol use while a 1975 survey of American high-school students reported that 90 percent of them used alcohol; 14 percent to the point of abuse. Some researchers estimate problem drinking among high-school students at 50 percent. In general, lower socioeconomic groups show higher proportions of problem drinkers than do higher socioeconomic groups. A 1977 survey of the Indian adolescent population reported that 78 percent had tried alcohol (versus 53 percent of the U. S. population) while 60 percent (versus 20 percent) had used it recently.

Hammerschlag, C.A. "American Indian Disenfranchise-ment: Its Impact on Health and Health Care," White Cloud Journal of American Indian Mental Health. 2 (4): 32-36, 1982.

The author describes how American Indians have been historically deprived of their rights as citizens, and the impact of this disenfranchisement on their health and health care. It is reported that alcoholism rates among American Indians range from 50 to 90 percent.   8 Ref.

Harford, Thomas C. ed.; Gaines, Lawrence S. ed.   Social Drinking Contexts.   Proceedings of a Workshop. (Washington,D.C.   September 17-19, 1979).   Research Monograph No. 7.   Rockville, Md.:   National Institute on Alcohol Abuse and Alcoholism, 1981.

This monograph presents the proceedings of a workshop on the contexts of social drinking, i.e.   the situational factors associated with drinking which might increase or inhibit heavier consumption.   A brief foreword, participant list, and editors' introduction are   presented   followed   by   the   13   workshop presentations; which include chapters such as "The Context of Native American Drinking: What We Know So Far", by Joy Leland; and "There's a Place for Everything and Everything in Its Place: Environmental Influences on Urban Indian Drinking Patterns", by Joan Weibel.

Heath, D. B. "Alcohol Use Among North American Indians,"   In: R.G. Smart, et al. (eds.), Research Advances in Alcohol and Drug Problems.   New York, N.Y.: Plenum Press, 1983.   472 p. (pp. 343-396).

A general introduction to the range of beliefs and behaviors that are associated with alcohol use among North American Indians, and the ways in which those beliefs and behaviors relate to understanding other aspects of Indian life is provided.   Historical perspective is important both because the dynamics of interethnic relations often played a crucial role in terms of the context in which Indians learned to drink, and because the dynamics of change in other aspects of culture are often reflected in changing patterns of alcohol use and meanings.   Brief analysis of the fire-water   myths   dispels   erroneous   stereotypes. Ethnographic and regional variation underscores the reality of social and cultural diversity among Indians. Aspects of health and social welfare are summarized in terms of current usage that emphasizes the problem aspects.   A brief review of epidemiology, physiological morbidity, mental health, homicide and suicide, acci-dents, sudden death, arrests, family and group disruption, and adjustment and adaptation is provided. A discussion of treatment and related issues demon-strates the practical implications of such knowledge, while theoretic issues help relate the Indian data to worldwide perspectives on alcohol use, its meanings, and its consequences.   Topics include stress and anomie, dependency, power, social organization, and the importance of sociocultural differences.   290 Ref.

Holmgren, C., Fitzgerald, B. J., Carman, Roderick S. "Alienation and Alcohol Use by American Indian and Caucasian High School Students," Journal of Social Psychology 120; 1, 1983.

The purpose of this study was to determine the relationship between student drinking patterns and alienation. 114 Indian students and 328 Caucasian students were given a questionnaire. Results indicated that the Indian students experienced a significantly higher incidence of alienation and this finding supports a basic assumption of the study, that an individual's position in the social system has significant consequences for psychological adjustment.

Horton, James M., Annolora, Donald J. "Student Dropout Study of Fort Wingate, New Mexico High School," BIA Education Research Bulletin, 3, 1974, 14 pgs.

This report examined the American Indian dropout rate for the Fall semester, 1973-1974, at Ft. Wingate High School (FWHS) in Gallup, New Mexico. For the period, the FWHS dropout rate was 26 percent, compared to a national average of about 25 percent (FWHS statistics are for one semester; national statistics are for an entire year). Dropouts were later defined as students who had enrolled in the Federal boarding school and later withdrew without completing a full year. Reasons for leaving were: (1) illness, (2) transferred to another school, (3) did not return from home leave, and (4) some kind of trouble. A questionnaire was developed and sent out to each of the identified dropouts, with a 35.4 percent return rate. Section A asked reasons for withdrawal, covering health, absence, parental influence, dorm conditions, and trouble with police, other students, or at home. The major reasons for dropping out were: (1) sent home for drinking or AWOL (17.2 percent); (2) stealing in dorms (16.6 percent); and (3) missed too many days. Things the respondents liked most about FWHS were counselors (92.7 percent), teachers (91.2 percent), and activities (90.6 percent). Activities and classes were felt to be the best things about Wingate High School; drinking and stealing in the dorms were the worst. (SHB)

Idaho State Journal   "Indian Alcoholism May Be Overstated Myth," Pocatello, Ill.: 18 Aug 1982.

It is contended that the current statistics commonly cited for alcoholism among Indians are grossly misleading. Three questions which must be asked in determining the rate of the problem are based on definitions of: (1) individual drinking, (2) tribal drinking, and (3) Indian drinking. Alcoholism among

Indians is thus a collection of problems. Recent research and proposals for future research are discussed.

Jaranson, James, M.; Gregory, Delores C.   "Job Satisfaction in the Portland Area Indian Health Service," White Cloud Journal. 1980, vol 1(4),   20-28.

Administered   in   the   Minnesota   Satisfaction Questionnaire to 299 Portland area Indian Health Service employees. Overall, SS were satisfied with their jobs. Those who qualified for Indian preference were more satisfied with their chances for advancement. Women and Indians were underrepresented in the higher civil service grades and in the commissioned corps. Nonclinical employees and those working longer in federal systems were more satisfies. 15 Ref.

Jilek, W.G.   "Anomic Depression, Alcoholism and a Culture Congenial Indian Response." Journal of Studies on Alcohol.

Statistical data are presented on the prevalence of alcohol-related problems among the general and Indian populations of British Columbia, Canada in 1973. It is reported that in 1975, 20.9 percent of the inmates incarcerated   for   criminal   homicide   in   federal correctional institutions in the lower mainland of British   Columbia   were   Indians,   noting   that   the homicidal act was always alcohol-related, in most cases under directly verified intoxication, and that victims were   mostly   Indians.   Findings   from   psychiatric observations of the Fraser Valley population of British Columbia indicate that alcoholism and depression were more prevalent among the Coast Salish Indians than among any other cultural group. The development of anomic depression among these Canadian Indians is described. It is noted that this type of depression is usually associated with alcohol or drug abuse, and is a reaction to alienation from aboriginal culture under westernizing influences. Traditional Indian spirit dances and ceremonies are also described, and their use as a form of psychotherapy for anomic depression and alcoholism is discussed. 20 Ref.

Jilek, Aall, L.   "Acculturation, Alcoholism and Indian-style Alcoholics Anonymous," Journal of Studies on Alcohol.

A brief introduction to traditional Coast Salish Indian culture is presented to explain why this population has been particularly vulnerable to the impact of Western ways of life, including the use of alcohol. Problems associated with alcohol encountered by these Indians in their attempt to cope with the dominant white culture are discussed. The roles of Alcoholics Anonymous (AA) and church organizations in helping Coast Salish Indians with alcohol problems is described, emphasis is on how, based on the Indians' own initiative, the incorporation of Indian culture on AA has helped develop a successful antialcoholism program. It is contended that only when the Indian people can regain their cultural identity and self-respect will they have the inner strength necessary to fight alcoholism. 29 Ref.

Klinekole, Ruth V. "Indian Students' Problems in Boarding Schools," BIA Education Research Bulletin, 7, 1979, pp. 16-25.

This study presents a discussion of problems faced by Indian students who attend boarding schools. Utilizing data gathered through previous surveys, the author presents documentation to support each of the specific difficulties described in the article. Specific problems explicated include adaptation to a new environment, alcohol abuse, conflicting student/system goals, and rule compliance. Characteristics of students attending the boarding schools as well as their reasons for attending are also presented. Statistics are also presented in relation to the quality of the education provided in the institutions.

Kraus, Robert, F.; Buffler, Patricia, A. "Sociocultural Stress and the American Native in Alaska: An Analysis of Changing Patterns of Psychiatric Illness and Alcohol Abuse Among Alaska Natives," Culture, Medicine and Psychiatry. (3), 1979, 111-151.

Selected morbidity and mortality statistics are used to show the current status and developing trends of psychiatric illness and alcohol abuse among the Aleut, Athabascan, Yupik, Inupiat, Tlingit, Haida, and Tsimpshian. The records of the various health services centers shows that Alaska Natives have a higher rate in each category of violent death, suicide, homicide, accidents, and alcohol that Alaska non-natives, American Indians and the U.S. (all races) and are rising. Behavioral disturbance and violent death are the primary elements of this public health problem.

Lake, R.G. "Discussion of native American Health Problems, Needs, and Services, with a Focus on Northwestern California," White Cloud Journal of American Indian Mental Health. 2(4): 23-31. 1982.

The author discusses Native American health problems (including alcohol abuse and alcoholism), needs, and services, and contends that these problems (physical and mental) are directly related to the way in which the white mainstream culture has historically mistreated Native Americans. Some objectives that need to be met to resolve these problems are presented. 43 Ref.

Leland, J. North American Indian Drinking and Alcohol Abuse, Reno, Nevada: Desert Research Institute, University of Nevada System, 1977, 145 pgs.

The indicators used for assessing the extent of problem drinking among Indians are by necessity mostly indirect. Literature is reviewed on alcohol as it relates to Indian suicide, accidental death, homicide, crime, cirrhosis, and youth. Other topics discussed include: (1) the fetal alcohol syndrome; (2) alcohol use by urban Indians; (3) why Indians drink (physical and cultural explanations), and social deprivation); (4) treatment of alcohol abuse; and (5) research. 296 Ref.

Leland, Joy "Alcohol, Anthropologists and Native Americans," Human Organization. 38 (1), Spring, 1979, pp. 94-99.

A brief history of the transfer of the Indian Alcohol programs from the jurisdiction of the National Institute on Alcohol Abuse and Alcoholism (NIAAA) to the Indian Health Services (IHS) is presented, and the advantages and disadvantages of this event are summarized. Comparisons are made between Indian and other NIAAA-sponsored treatment projects. The authors also highlight the significant but generally unobtrusive influence that anthropologists have had on the establishment of policy in Indian alcohol matters. Their impact on the literature is considered to be most evident in the emphasis on cultural relativity and the need for self-determination in dealing with alcohol-related problems among American Indians.

Lemert, E.M. "Drinking Among American Indians," In: E.L. Gomberg, et al., (eds.) Alcohol, Science and Society Revisited. Ann Arbor, Mi.: University of Michigan Press, 1982. 440 p. pp. 80-95.

It is contended that American Indians, perhaps more than any other population, are celebrated in fact and fiction for their misadventures with alcohol. Several research studies are cited that challenge the historical portrayal of orgiastic drunkenness among American Indians and insist that this picture has been overdrawn.   General theoretical considerations in studies of drinking behavior among American Indians are addressed, and Indian drinking patterns are described. The prevalence of alcoholism among this population is discussed, including concomitants of, and various explanations given for Indian drinking.   The influence of cultural stereotypes of Indian drinking is also discussed.   It is concluded that the evidence on drinking by American Indians appears to favor adoption of a sociocultural model to explain this behavior; however, its construction remains to be accomplished. Granting that social structure, patterned behavior, traditions, and cultural symbols help to shape the drinking habits of Indians, certain of its aspects require attention to subjective processes to be fully understood.   36 Ref.

Liban, C. B., Smart, R. G.   "Drinking and Drug Use Among Ontario Indian Students,"   Drug and Alcohol Dependence, 9 (2):   161-171, 1982.

From a sample of Ontario students in grades seven through thirteen, 64 students of Native Indian parentage were successfully matched with 64 non-Indian students on five demographic variables.   A comparison of alcohol and drug use among the two groups suggested that Indian students use alcohol and drugs in a manner similar to that of their peers in the same geographical location and of similar socioeconomic background.   12 Ref.

Locklear, Von Sevastion.   "A Cross Cultural Study to Determine How Mental Health is Defined in a Tri-racial County in Southeastern North Carolina (American Indian Lumbee)," Dissertation.   The Ohio State University, 1985, 316 p.

The purpose of this study was to determine how mental health is defined in a tri-racial county in southeastern North Caroline, composed of one American Indian tribe (Lumbee) and white and black residents. The focus of this study was the Lumbee Indian definition of mental health.This was an exploratory, descriptive study.   Employing the key informant approach, 60 subjects (20 of each racial group) were nominated and subsequently selected to serve as key informants.   The researcher developed an instrument to collect the data.   The means of data collection was a tape-recorded personal interview by the researcher, guided by a questionnaire.   The data was analyzed utilizing content analysis.

This study found that there were differences as well as similarities in the way mental health was defined by the three racial groups. Although similar themes were identified by all three racial groups, there were varying degrees of emphasis that each group placed on these themes in their definitions of mental health. The study found that all three racial groups believed that there was a higher level of tolerance for behaviors such as alcoholism, "fist fighting," domestic violence, and drug abuse among the Lumbee Indian community. Another difference that was found among the Lumbee Indians which affected their definition of mental health included an identified relationship between mental and physical health (mind/body holism). The study also found that there was apparent confusion between mental health and mental illness and perceptions or racial differences in the definition of mental health among all three racial groups. Factors such as age, income and gender were found to be important in the definition of mental health. In addition, the study identified a number of factors as contributors to the promotion and maintenance of mental health, particularly within the Lumbee Indian community. For example, the study found that the Lumbee Indians do not use the formal mental health system, but rely on natural support systems within the community (e.g., family, Lumbee Indian elders, friends and clergy) for solving mental health problems and promoting mental health.

Longie, J. D. "Alcohol and American Indian Children: An Assessment of Attitudes and Behavior," Dissertation. Dissertation Abstracts International, 44(11): 3328-A, 1984.

The attitudes and behavior of preadolescent Indian children toward alcohol use were studied here. Results of a study indicated eight children had alcoholic beverage consumption experience, 18 children would try drinking in the future, and 44 of them had not and would not drink. In both reservation areas and the rural nonreservation community, the majority of children were strictly nondrinkers, while in the urban areas the majority of children were drinkers or potential drinkers. By age twelve, positive predispositions toward drinking clearly predominated, with drinkers and potential drinkers outnumbering nondrinkers three to one.

May, P.A. "Substance Abuse and American Indians: Prevalence and Susceptibility," International Journal of the Addictions. 17(7): 1185-1209, 1982.

The use of alcohol and other substances by American Indians has received considerable popular attention over the years. Empirical studies of prevalence for all types of substance abuse, however, have generally been few and limited in scope. Prevalence studies among Indians are reviewed and analyzed by comparison with each other and with national studies. Issues important to the research of Indian alcohol and drug abuse are discussed. A scheme of susceptibility which may explain the patterns of variation in both tribal and individual substance abuse is proposed. 40 Ref.

May, P. A. "Susceptibility to Substance Abuse Among American Indians: Variation Across Sociocultural Settings," Conference Paper, 43rd Annual Scientific Meeting of the Committee on Problems of Drug Dependence, San Francisco, CA: 12-15, July, 1981. 561 p. (pp. 34-44), 1982.

The author contends that, in spite of the considerable attention given to Indian drinking, insights into prevalence, incidence, variation of patterns, and susceptibility to alcohol intoxication and dependence were slow in developing. In this paper, the prevalence and incidence of drinking among Indians are examined and a few selective works on Indian drinking are used to illustrate topics vital to the understanding of susceptibility to all types of substance abuse. It is concluded that: (1) slightly higher levels of adolescent years; (2) many Indian peer groups define alcohol, inhalants, and marijuana as acceptable, but for most young Indians the usage of drugs other than alcohol is an experimental, transitory behavior; (3) individuals who are well integrated into and identify with both modern and traditional Indian customs are the least susceptible to drug abuse, while those who are not well established in any socially integrated role in either white or Indian society are the most likely to abuse drugs and to continue their use. 28 Ref.

McBride, D. C. and Page, J. B. "Adolescent Indian Substance Abuse: Ecological and Sociocultural Factors," Youth and Society, 2(4): 475-492, 1980.

Historical evidence of substance (including alcohol) abuse among American Indians is briefly discussed. Available epidemiological data on the extent and type of abuse are reviewed, and the sociocultural explanations of Indian substance abuse patterns are examined. The current state of the treatment intervention services directed toward Indian substance abusers is assessed. 42 Ref.

McDonald, D.R. Tulapai to Tokay: A Bibliography of Alcohol Use and Abuse Among Native Americans of North America. New Haven, CT.: HRAF Press, 1980. 356 p.

This bibliography provides an overview of the literature concerning alcohol use by Native Americans in the annotations, and a guide to a more detailed reading on specific topics in the comprehensive indes. Please see in particular "Adolescents" (p.317) and "Youth" (p. 356 in the index.

Miller, S. K.; Helmick, E. F.: McClure, W. T. "Adolescent Alcoholism: A Relationship to Other Mental Health Problems," Currents in Alcoholism Vol. IB. New York: Grune and Stratton, 1978. 498 p. (pp. 77-85).

In 1974, the Alaska Native Health Board in cooperation with the staff and students of the Mt. Edgecumbe Boarding School and others, undertook a study directed at answering some questions concerning the magnitude of the drinking problem among Native Alaskan students, the age and sex distribution, and the causes of alcohol abuse in this population. A total of 359 of a possible 532 students were evaluated. This evaluation revealed 105 students who, counselors felt, had an alcohol problem of some severity. The maximum estimate of alcohol abuse prevalence was 29 percent (105/359). The students who had drinking problems were similar in age and sex to those with no drinking problems although slightly fewer females were in the alcohol abuse group. Causal conclusions were not drawn in this study.   3 Ref.

Mueller, Julie M.   "The Image of the Native American in Young Adult Fiction (1960-1975)," Master's Thesis, university of Chicago, 1986, 71 p.

The portrayal of the American Indian in young adult fiction was studied through the examination of 23 works of realistic or historical fiction published from 1960 to 1985. Books selected from the card catalogue at the Center for Children's Books at the University of Chicago were primarily about Indians or Indian life, and were appropriate for readers at grade 7 or above. All selections were read and analyzed to determine trends in the portrayal of the American Indian. Analysis included diversity of the literature, types of themes and issues, story settings, tribes, and main characters. Results showed significant changes in the image of the American Indian in the years under study. From 1970 to 1979 works available grew in diversity, and story settings become more varied and realistic. Alcoholism was the most frequently discussed issue in books from the 1960's, but later works looked at broader range of issues including feminism and ecology. The portrayal of tribes moved from traditional and conservative in the 1960's to greater accuracy and diversity in the 1980's.   There is still a need to improve accuracy in many areas of the works studied and a need for more literature by American Indian authors.

Negrete, Juan C. "Cultural Aspects of Alcohol and Drug Problems in Canada," National Institute on Drug Abuse: Research Monograph Series. 1982, Research Monograph 43 21-35. Rockville, Md., 1982.

Compares patterns of drug and alcohol problems among the various ethnic groups and provinces of Canada and with the patterns reported for comparable groups and areas of the US. Although alcohol consumption is similar in the US and Canada, differences are noted in relation to the existence of a large French minority and the larger proportion of Native Americans in Canada. Alcohol-related social problems such as driving offenses and aggressive behavior are shown to reflect regional and ethnic differences, community attitudes toward drinking, and differential police action--particularly toward Native Americans. Opiate and Methadone abuse are a smaller problem in Canada than in the US., although use of psychotropics is higher in Canada. (15 Ref.).

Noble, Ernest P., (ed.) Third Special Report to the U.S. Congress on Alcohol and Health, Washington, D. C.: Government Printing Office, 1978. 98 P.

This report incorporates the most significant findings of recent research in the field of alcoholism. The findings are described in extensive detail in support of the third special report on alcohol and health. The report highlights: (1) prevalence and patterns of alcohol use, (2) alcohol use and abuse among special population groups, (3) biomedical consequences of alcohol use and abuse (4) the fetal alcohol syndrome and other effects on offspring, (5) interaction of alcohol and other drugs, (6) psychological effects of alcohol, (7) genetic and family factors relating to alcoholism, (8) alcohol-related accidents, crime and violence, (9) treatment of alcoholism and problem drinking, (10) occupational alcoholism programming, (11) financing alcoholism treatment services, and (12) the prevention of alcohol problems. Youth and American Indians are discussed here.

Oetting, E. R., Beauvais, F. "A Typology of Adolescent Drug Use: A Practical Classification System Journal Citation," Academic Psychology Bulletin, 5; 1, 1983.

The purpose of this study was to devise a hierarchical system of classifying American Indian and Non-Indian drug users by pattern and type. Eight different types were discerned: each type relates specifically to an individual's social and personal characteristics as well as the degree of seriousness of his or her drug problem. This was edited to be understandable to a non-scientist.

Oetting, E. R.; and others "Drug use among Native American Youth: Summary of findings (1975 - 1981)," Rockville, MD.: National Institute on Drug Abuse, 1982. ERIC ED 230341.

Drug use among 4-6 and 7-12 grade American Indian youth attending reservation schools was studied utilizing anonymous self-report surveys administered in class by non-school personnel. The children's survey asked about use of alcohol, marijuana, inhalants, and pills. The adolescent survey included these drugs plus eight other commonly abused drugs. Information was obtained on lifetime and current use, intensity and patterns of use, and correlates of drug use (e.g., demographics, and attitudes toward drugs and the future, peer and family influence, general deviance, cultural identification, school adjustment, and personal adjustment). Clustered into three separate periods to allow examination of drug use over time, data were collected on over 9,000 Indian students. Indian adolescents in grades 7-12 had a higher exposure level to every drug included in the survey; inhalants were tried more often by Indian youth; Indian children appeared to start use of marijuana and inhalants at a young age, and identification with Indian culture provided some protection against the more serious types of drug involvement.

Oetting, E.R.; Beauvais, F. Drug Use Among Native American Youth: Summary of Findings 1975-1981. Fort Collins, Co.: Colorado State University, 1982. 123 p.

A summary of the present state of knowledge about the extent of drug use among Native American youth is presented. Drug involvement among Indian youth is very high, particularly for marijuana, but also for alcohol, inhalants, and stimulants. Indian people are subject to many pressures, both current and historical, which may contribute to chemical abuse. These pressures include prejudice, poverty, and political wardship.

Oetting, E. R., Edwards, R., Goldstein, G. S., Garcia-Mason, V. "Drug Use Among Adolescents of Five Southwestern Native American Tribes," International Journal of the Addictions, 15(3): 439-445, 1980.

Drug use by Native American adolescents from five Southwestern tribes is compared with a large national sample. Native Americans show higher use of alcohol, marijuana, and inhalants from the 7th through 12th grade. They show lower use of barbiturates. Peyote may be seen less dangerous that LSD. There are no significant differences for other drugs. Cultural characteristics that may influence potential danger from drug use and intervention strategies are noted. 7 Ref.

Oetting, E. R., and Goldstein, G. S. "Drug Use Among Native American Adolescents," Youth Drug Abuse, Lexington, MA.:   D.C. Heath, 1979. 681 p. (pp. 409-441).

A report is presented on drug (including alcohol) use in Native American adolescent populations. Drug problems are reviewed in the context of such factors as cultural heritage, the acculturation process, multiple life problems, and the impoverished socioeconomic conditions of the six tribes studied in several southwestern states. Drug use prevalence rates are compared with those reported in a nationally representative sample to show the differences in drug involvement. Native American drug users are also compared with peers who do not use drugs, on the personal and social characteristics, values, and attitudes towards the major social institutions in their lives. 18 Ref.

Oetting, E. R. and Goldstein, G. S. Native American Drug Use, Ft. Collins, Co.: Colorado State University, Department of Psychology, 1977, 88 p.

The second final report on the investigation of drug misuse among Indian adolescents is presented. An expanded sample of nearly 3000 adolescents from 14 different tribes nationwide were used in this study. These adolescents were found to show two to three times the amount of drug experimentation than was found in a large sample of other adolescents. In particular, considerably more use of marijuana, inhalants and alcohol was noted. Drug use patterns were found to be related to peer influence, broken family structures, isolation from societal institutions such as church and school, and feelings that life is going to be a failure. 6 Ref.

Oetting, E. R., Goldstein, G. S., Beauvais, F., et. al., Drug Abuse Among Indian Children, Fort Collins, CO.: Colorado State University, Department of Psychology, 1980.

This interim report on drug use among nine to twelve year old Native Americans is part of a series of in-depth studies. A review of previous studies on drug use by Native American adolescents is presented. The present study, using a sample of over 1,000 subjects, indicates that drug use is high among these children. It is indicated that by the time these children reached 12 years of age they had used marijuana, inhalants, and alcohol more than the average for a national sample of children who were much older (12 to 17 years). Drug use and correlates are discussed including implications for future drug use. A copy of the survey questionnaire is provided.

Olsen, L. K., and Baffi, C. R. "Descriptive Analysis of Drug and Alcohol Use Among Selected Native American High School Students," Journal of Drug Education 12(2): 97-102, 1982.

Self-reported alcohol and drug use among selected Native American high school students was analyzed. The results showed that 83.6 percent reported having experimented with alcohol, and an additional 43 percent reported using some combination of alcohol and other drugs on a regular basis. Native American students appear to use alcohol and drugs at levels similar to those of their non-Native American counterparts. It is suggested that educators initiate programs which will enhance student self-esteem and decision making skills and result in a decrease in students' alcohol and drug abuse. 4 Ref.

Porche, M. "Alcohol Abuse Concerns and Needs of Minority Populations," Conference Paper, National Council on Alcoholism 29th Annual Forum. New Orleans, LA: 12 April, 1981.

The social correlates of alcohol abuse in relation to minority populations are described. These minority populations include Blacks, females, teenagers, elderly, Spanish speaking individuals, and Native American Indians. Topics covered in this paper include demographic characteristics, incidents and outcomes, unique needs and concerns, treatment modalities, preventive measures, and research findings. 20 Ref.

Poulson, R. L., Pettibone, T. J., Willey, D. S. "Ethnic Variables and Problem Drinking in a Select Sample of Southwestern Two-year Multicultural College Students," American Journal of Drug and Alcohol Abuse, 5(4): 497-506, 1978.

Five hundred and ninety-two Anglo, Mexican American, and American Indian students from nine selected two-year colleges in the Southwest were given a self-administered questionnaire with items related to problem drinking (dependent variable) and various

social, psychological, and demographic information
(independent variables).   Analyses included
discriminant analysis, chi square, and etc. While
ethnicity per se contributed little to the
discrimination of problem from nonproblem drinkers,
several other variables provided an overall correct
classification (discrimination) rate of 79.73 percent.
These variable were, in order of discriminating power:
neighborhood people drink, veteran status, live life
differently, close friend with drinking problem, drink
because acquaintances drink, and age. It is
hypothesized that the psychological principle of
individual differences, and the significance of some
other study variables, may have overshadowed any ethnic
effect. Measurement problems in this area are
discussed as well as some potential research
directions. 20 Ref.

Rachal-J-Valley; Hubbard-Robert,L.; Williams, Jay, R.;
Tuchfeld, Barry B."Drinking Levels and Problem Drinking
among Junior and Senior High-School Students," Journal
of Studies on Alcohol 37(11), Nov. 1976, 1751-1761.

The basic data and operational definitions developed by
the Research Triangle Institute (RTI), in a national
study of adolescent drinking behavior, are described.
The measurements and classifications of adolescent
drinking developed in the study, application of these
to indicate levels of adolescent drinking, and the
operational definition of problem drinking and its
relation to other variables, are discussed. The study
was based on a nationwide probability sample of all
junior and senior high-school students in the
continuous forty-eight states. A self administered
thirty-five page questionnaire was completed by the
sample respondents during one class period on a regular
school day. Usable questionnaires were obtained from
13,122 respondents (72.7 percent response rate).
Self-report ethnic classifications found: 69.1 percent
white, 11.5 percent Spanish-American, 7.1 percent
black, 6.1 percent American Indian, 1.7 percent
Oriental, and 4.5 percent other. Two tables.
Modified Authors' Summary.

Rachal, J.V.; Williams, J.R.; Brehm, M.L.; Cavenaugh,
B.: Moore, P.P. and Eckerman, W.C. National Study of
Adolescent Drinking Behavior, Attitudes and Correlates,
Final Report. (Prepared for the National Institute on
Alcohol Abuse and Alcoholism). Springfield, VA.: U.S.
National Technical Information Service, 1975, 208 p.

This report on adolescent alcohol abuse is based on
self-administered questionnaires given to a random
sample of high school students in 1974. The study

presents the relationship between adolescent drinking
behavior and selected characteristics (Type of
beverage, race, sex, age, religion, urban or nonurban
residents, occupation of parents, parental and peer
drinking habits, drug experience, and GPA).

Royce, J. E. "Special Groups" Alcohol Problems and
Alcoholism: A Comprehensive Survey, New York: The
Free Press, 1981, 383 p. (pp. 103-118).

The alcohol problems of women, youth, the elderly,
racial minorities (American Indians, Blacks, Hispanics,
Asian-Americans), the military, Skid Row alcoholics and
other special groups (physicians, clergy) are
discussed. In considering the problems of youth, a
distinction is made between drinking and alcoholism and
the ways in which adolescent alcoholism differs from
adult alcoholism are noted.

Rush, B., and Ogborne, A. (Eds.) Evaluation Research
in the Canadian Addictions Field: Proceedings of the
2nd Annual Meeting of the Special Interest Group on
Program Evaluation of the Canadian Addiction
Foundation, Regina, Saskatchewan, Canada: 8-9
September 1982. 184 pgs.

Papers presented at the Second Annual Meeting of the
Special Interest Group on Program Evaluation (SIGPF.),
Canadian Addiction Foundation are provided. These
papers represent a limited set of the diverse topics
and issues confronting evaluators practicing in
Canadian addiction (alcohol and drug abuse) programs.
Session topics include: (1) client information systems;
(2) self-help groups, specifically, Alcoholics
Anonymous (AA) and program evaluation; (3) evaluating
media campaigns; and (4) evaluation and programs for
native peoples of Canada.

Saslow, Harry L. "Alcoholism: The Family and Child
Personality of the Native American." Paper read at the
American Psychological Association, September 8, 1972.

Schecter, A. J. (Ed.) Drug dependence and Alcoholism.
Volume 2: Social and Behavioral Issues, New York, NY:
Plenum Press, 1981. 1041 p.

In volume two of a two-volume series of papers
presented at the 1978 National Drug Abuse Conference,
papers concerned with social and behavioral aspects of
alcohol and drug abuse are provided. The following
topics are addressed: (1) minorities and special needs;
(2) rural and urban issues; (3) prevention; (4)
training, education, and credentialing; (5) vocational
rehabilitation; (6) managerial and administrative

issues;   (7) sociology of drug   abuse   (including alcoholism); and (8) public policy. The first volume of the series focused on biomedical issues.

Schmalz, Peter Stanley.   "The Ojibwa of Southern Ontario."   Ph.D. Dissertation.   University of Waterloo (Canada) 1985,

This dissertation is intended to illustrate the rise and fall of the southern Ontario Ojibwa through three periods involving the French, English, and Canadian governments, respectively. Disease, liquor and wars against the United States were related factors in their decline. The appendix, "Education", examines the weaknesses of the assimilationist policy established for the Ojibwa children and gives some hope for the future in an Ojibwa renaissance if they are treated as 'citizens plus' and are permitted to control their own education.

Segal, R. (eds.) Proceedings of the 1981 Annual School on Alcohol and Addiction Studies. University of Alaska, Center for Alcohol and Addiction Studies, 1981. Anchorage, Alaska.

Proceedings of workshops held at the 1981 Annual School on Alcohol and Addiction Studies are presented, focusing on treatment issues in Alaska, a multicultural and changing society. This program was concerned with helping to expand the awareness of human services providers and others regarding the nature and impact of alcohol and other drugs. The many different factors that impact effective treatment, intervention, and prevention of substance abuse are discussed.

Segal, B. "Alcohol and Alcoholism in Alaska: Research in a Multicultural and Transitory Society," International Journal of the Addictions. 18(3): 379-392, 1983.

An overview of Alaska and its people is provided, including geographical and climatic features, its native and nonnative people, and economic and social changes. Specifically, research in Alaska concerning alcohol use by Native Alaskans is reviewed, in particular, issues involved when traditional cross-cultural research procedures are followed. Questions are raised concerning what the focus of this research might be, and suggestions for more culturally relevant research are advanced. 12 Ref.

Senay, E.C. "Special Populations," In: E.C. Senay, Substance Abuse Disorders in Clinical Practice. Boston, MA.: John Wright, 1983. 243 p. (pp. 175-189).

The term "special populations; has been coined to
indicate that substance (including alcohol) and the
abuse of same in a given group who have unique
characteristics that, for best results, must be taken
into account in diagnosis and treatment. The following
groups are described as special populations because of
their characteristics and treatment needs: elderly,
women, gays and lesbians, handicapped persons,
Hispanics, Blacks, American Indians, Asian Americans,
and impaired physicians. 19 Ref.

Simeone, C. M. "Take Over Cycle: An Epidemiological
Approach to Indian Drinking in Alaska," Conference
paper, Twenty-fifth International Institute on the
Prevention and Treatment of Alcoholism, Tours, France:
18-22 June 1979, 516 p. (pp. 500-503). Published in
A.J. Schecter, Ed., Drug Dependence and Alcoholism,
Vol. 2: Social and Behavioral Issues. New York:
Plenum Press, 1981, 1041 p. (pp. 597-600).

The Take Over Cycle is a drinking ritual that is a
substitute method of fulfilling the obligations of
values traditionally served by the Potlatch.
Historically, the cultural values of social activity,
reciprocity, prestige, and spiritual regeneration were
fulfilled through the Potlatch. The people involved in
the Potlatch and Take Over Cycle are athabascan
speaking people from the Upper Tanana and upper Copper
River regions of eastern interior Alaska. The Take
Over Cycle is the ongoing and dynamic transfer of the
activity of drinking from one individual or group to
another individual or group in a specific time and a
specific geographic region. One of several drinkers
will drink from two days to two weeks and then one or
several others will "take over" the drinking. The
drinking in the village and region never stops. An
epidemiological analysis of problem drinking caused by
this Take Over Cycle is presented. 3 Ref.

Staats, Elmer B. Progress and Problems in providing
Health Services to Indians, Report to the Congress.
Washington, D.C., Government Accounting Office, 1974.

A report to the Congress on Indian health care is
focused on the following health problems: 1) Maternal
and child health; 2) Otitis media (inflammation of the
middle ear); 3) Tuberculosis; 4) venereal disease; and
5) Alcoholism and alcohol abuse. It is speculated that
alcoholism adversely influences more aspects of
American Indian lives than any other health problem.
Most accidents, homicides, assaults, and suicide
attempts have been associated with drinking. The
author concludes that Indian health remains
significantly worse than that of the general

population, with substantial adverse effects on the individual, the family, and the community. It is recommended that the Secretary of HEW develop through the Indian Health Service, ways to identify the extent of the alcohol problem, influence funding sources for programs needed at specific locations, and establish procedures for the referral of alcoholic patients to rehabilitation programs.

Stanchfield, A. D. "Myths, Misconceptions and Misinformation About Alcohol or, Tequila Isn't the Only Alcohol to Take with a Grain of Salt," Ph.D. Dissertation, The Florida State University, 1979.

Myths related to alcohol are exemplified by attitudes, demographic groupings, reasons for use, physical effects, social effects and relationships, and individual and group disorganization. Factors influencing the creation and continuation of myths include emotion (as opposed to logic), generalizations from observation, explanations of observations, social control, and the influence of "Authorities" including the "Reformed Reformer" (The Ex-Alcoholic). Under demographic groupings, early interest in and use of alcohol, teenage preferences, stability of drinking patterns, drinking and drug use by women, misconceptions about the poor, the black and American Indian, are discussed. Reasons for use range from instinct and positive ideas about pleasure and effect, to negative ideas of abnormality, suicide, rebellion, anomie and the invalidity of pleasure.

Stevens, S.M. "Alcohol and World View: A Study of Passamaquoddy Alcohol Use," Journal of Studies on Alcohol.

The historical and cultural settings of the Passamaquoddy Indians of Maine are described. The supernatural world view of these people is discussed, including how alcohol has been incorporated into this perspective. It is demonstrated how an effective alcoholism program for this population would ideally incorporate prevailing beliefs, noting that present programs do not, because of lack of awareness of these features by non-Indian program planners, a reluctance on the part of Passamaquoddy to expose their beliefs to possible ridicule, and a widespread Passamaquoddy view that "if the white man brought liquor, the white man knows how to cure alcoholics." 7 Ref.

Stratton, R.; Zeiner, Arthur R.; Parades, A. "Tribal Affiliation and Prevalence of Alcohol Problems," Journal of Alcohol Studies on Alcohol 1978 July vol. 39(7) 1166-1177.

Suggests the differences in tribal culture, history and settlement, may explain why Indians in Eastern Oklahoma have lower rates of alcohol-related arrests and deaths than do Indians in the Western part of the state. (26 Ref.).

Stratton, R. "Relationship Between Prevalence of Alcohol Problems and Socioeconomic Conditions Among Oklahoma Native Americans." In. M. Galanter, Ed., Currents in Alcoholism:... Volume VIII New York, NY.: Grune & Stratton, 1981. 527 p. (pp. 315-325).

Oklahoma Indian tribes are ranked according to five problem drinking indicators and five socioeconomic indices. The relationship between the tribes' prevalence of alcohol problems and socioeconomic conditions is examined. It was found that unfavorable socioeconomic conditions predicted high rates of alcohol problems, while more favorable conditions did not predict low rates. It is concluded that social controls may be more important than socioeconomic conditions in controlling alcohol problems among Oklahoma native Americans. 13 Ref.

Street, Pamela; Wood, Ronald; Chowenhill, Rita Alcohol Use Among Native Americans: A Selective Annotated Bibliography. Prepared for the California Office of Alcoholism. Social Research Group, May 1976. Available from the Department of General Services, Publications, P. O. Box 1015, North Highlands, Ca. 95660 ($2.00).

This is an annotated bibliography of selected publications on alcohol use among Native Americans. No index is provided.

Topper, M.D. "Drinker's Story: An Important but Often Forgotten Source of Data," Journal of Studies on Alcohol. Suppl. No. 9: 73-86, 1981.

Two rather different methodologies have been developed for the study of cultural patterns of alcohol use and misuse among minority cultures and subcultures. One approach the cultural-historical-statistical model, provides information on the development of cultural drinking patterns through time, and data on the general incidence of morbidity and mortality caused by these patterns. The other approach is based on cognitive anthropology and participant observation, and provides data that are essential for understanding the basic cultural beliefs about alcohol use and drinkers' views of the behavior in which they are participating. Both forms of data are necessary if alcoholism programs are to be successfully implemented among cultural minorities; however, the cognitive approach has not received a great deal of attention outside of anthropology. Drinking habits and patterns of Navajo Indians are used as examples to demonstrate that the rigorous utilization of the cognitive research methodology can produce data and interpretations that can be useful sources of input for the development of culturally oriented treatment programs for minority cultures. 21 Ref.

Topper, Martin D. "Drinking Patterns, Culture Changes, Sociability, and Navajo Adolescents," Addictive Diseases, 1(1): 97-116, 1974.

The author reviews changes in Navajo drinking patterns, especially among adolescents that have been brought about by both long-term developments in the reservation economy stemming from the 1920's and from a sharp increase in the amount of spending by all levels of government and by private industry on the reservation since 1960. The effect of the changes has led Navajo youth to attempt acculturation into the white man's world, which through its pressures causes a high level of frustration that results from the inability to achieve even a poverty-level living standard on the reservation. Drinking has become one of the ways to express this frustration. The continual tribal population growth balanced against the ability of the reservation to attract jobs and the failure of young Navajos to relocate successfully in cities presents a serious social problem particularly in reference to the excessive patterns already established in agency towns. 24 Ref.

Tribal American/Training Consultants Associated. National Institute on Alcohol Abuse and Alcoholism: American Indian Alcoholism Evaluation - Monitoring - Design Project. Rockville, Md.: 1974, 240 p.

The purpose of this study was to evaluate the data collection instruments, to revise the processing system, and to evaluate the analytical results based on data submitted by sixteen Native American Alcoholism programs.

Uecker, A.E.; Boutilier, L.R.; Richardson, E.H. "Indianism' and the 'Richardson Indian Culturalization Test', A Reply to Walker et al." Journal of Studies on Alcohol. 42 (1): 168-171, 1981.

The authors respond to a comment on a study they previously published which found that, while MMPI profiles of 40 Indian and 40 white alcoholic male veterans were similar, Indianism as measured by the

Richardson Indian Culturalization Test was significantly related to some of the Indian scores. They argue that the test can be used in a fair manner (though they agree that it does need to be revised on some items) and that the test does not enforce negative stereotypes of the Native American.

United States. Indian Health Service, Division of Resource Coordination, Office of Program Statistics. Selected Vital Statistics for Indian Health Service Areas and Service Units, 1972-1977. Rockville, Md.: Indian Health Service, 1978, 123 p.

This publication focuses on population characteristics by service area. Specifically, statistical summaries are presented for demographic natality, and mortality rates of American Indians and Alaskan Natives served in each geographic area. Population estimates used in calculations were derived from a straight line interpolation between decennial census years 1960 and 1970 for the years 1971 through 1974. From 1975 on a new method was used which utilized actual Indian vital statistics. The authors hope that this summary of statistical information will be useful to planners in the health care area. LAT

United States Bureau of Indian Affairs, Human Services Resources, Alcoholism Devastation for Indians: An Analysis of Pre-Class and Post-Class Test Scores, Aberdeen, S.D., 1979.

A 35-item test was given to 72 Indian students enrolled in a course on alcoholism, on course content (alcohol and the Indian people, the effects of alcohol, alcoholism) before and after the course. The test consisted of 15 multiple choice and 20 true-false questions. Test results were received for 103 pretests and 91 post-tests; of these, 21 pretests had no matching post-test, and 19 post-tests had no matching pretest. Every Student scored higher on the post-test than on the pretest. Students (N-27) who had 18 or less items correct on the pretest gained an average of 12.19 items correct on the post-test. Students (N-45) who had 19 or more items correct on the pretest gained an average of 9.82 items on the post-test.

United States Institute of Alcohol Abuse and Alcoholism, National Study of Adolescent Drinking Behavior, Attitudes and Correlates, Final Report by J. V. Rachal, et. al., Rockville, MD., 1975, 208 p.

This report on adolescent alcohol abuse is based on self-administered questionnaires given to a random sample of high school students in 1974. The study

presents the relationship between adolescent drinking
behavior and selected characteristics (type of
beverage, race, sex, age, religion, urban or nonurban
resident, occupation of parents, parental and peer
drinking habits, drug experience, and GPA.)

Vizenor, G. "Indian Alcoholics Are Individuals, Not
White Mice," Minneapolis Star and Tribune.
Minneapolis, Mn.: 23 Apr. 1982.

It is contended that about half of the Native American
tribal population is chemically dependent upon alcohol
or other drugs, and that another forty percent are
affected as families and relatives of these people.
Problem drinking and alcoholism are most prevalent
among those Indians who are least acculturated to urban
life. Two themes are said to be evident in tribal
alcohol consumption: (1) tribal alcohol ingestion is
somehow different from other drinking, and (2) in spite
of the problems and abuses, tribal imbibing has
positive aspects. Research results from recent
studies, explaining these and other theoretical
definitions of the drinking patterns of American
Indians, are discussed.

Waddel, J.O., "Place of the Cactus Wine Ritual in the
Papago Indian Ecosystem," In: A. Bharate, Ed., The
Realm of the Extra-Human: Ideas and Actions. The
Hague, Netherlands: Mouton, 1976. pp. 213-228.

The role of the cactus wine (nawait) ritual is examined
as a regulatory and communicational mechanism in the
Papago Indian ecosystem.

Waddell, J. O., Everett, M. W., eds. Drinking Behavior
Among Southwestern Indians: An Anthropological
Perspective, Tucson, AZ.: University of Arizona Press,
1980. 248 p.

An effort is made to demonstrate the useful application
of culturally meaningful techniques toward a practical
understanding of American Indian drinking. The intent,
organization, and content of this volume reflects the
authors' belief that a systematic comparison of
culturally meaningful descriptions and explanations of
drinking, as they are used locally, can make significant practical contributions to the self-management
of problem drinking by Native Americans themselves.
This volume is divided into the following parts: (1)
historical antecedents; (2) drinking patterns in four
southwest Native American societies; (3) assessments by
Native American observers and public health workers;
and (4) the native southwest, Native Americans, and
alcohol use; some comparative conclusions.

Walker, C. G.   "Influence of Parental Drinking Behavior
on That of Adolescent Native Americans,"   M. A. Thesis,
University of Washington, Seattle; 1976.

In a mail questionnaire study of 44 Native American
adolescents aged 12-20 (mean age 16; 29 girls), 31 (22
girls) reported ever drinking alcoholic beverages.
There were 6 infrequent, 6 light, 11 moderate and 8
heavy drinkers. The average age at initial drinking
was 13 for girls and 14 for boys, the order of beverage
preference was beer, wine and spirits, the quantity
consumed increased with age, over half reported
drinking moderately until they felt good, and one-third
reported never getting drunk. Three (1 girl) reported
drinking rapidly to get drunk, and 3 others (2 girls)
reported getting drunk 1-2 times per week. Only 3
adolescents reported having drinking-related problems
in the past 5 years, while 12 said their mothers had
had problems, and 10 said their fathers had had
problems. Arguing or fighting was the most frequently
reported problem, followed by arrests for driving while
under the influence.

Walker, R.D.; Cohen, F.G.; Walker,P.S.   " 'Indianism'
and the 'Richardson Indian Culturalization Test', "
Journal of Studies on Alcohol.   42(1): 163-167, 1981.

The Richardson Indian Culturalization Test is presented
and examined.   Problems with using this test are
outlined.   This test has been used previously in the
study of alcohol misuse and treatment outcome among
American Indians.

Wanberg, Kenneth; Lewis, Ron; Foster, Mark L.
"Alcoholism and Ethnicity: A Comparative Study of
Alcohol Use Patterns Across Ethnic Groups,"
International Journal of the Addictions 13(8), 1978,
pp. 1245-1262.

This article focused on sociological and alcohol use
patterns in American Indian, black, Hispanic and white
Anglo groups of alcoholism patients of the Alcoholism
Division of the Fort Logan Mental Health Center,
located in Denver, Colorado.   In order to determine
sociological variables as well as alcohol use patterns,
the inventories which were routinely administered to
all patients as part of a data base were analyzed
concerning 70 American Indians, 47 blacks, 77 Hispanos
and 74 white Anglos (Total N=268).   Results of the
study showed that all groups experienced social and
vocational disruption, the American Indian experiencing
the greatest disruption of the four groups.   While the
four groups did not differ as to reasons for alcohol
use, American Indians and Hispanics were found "To

deviate gregariously, to drink more, and to have more disruption in social functioning." DAR

Weibel-Orlando, J.   "Substance Abuse Among American Indian Youth: A Continuing Crisis."   Journal of Drug Issues, 14(2):   313-335, 1984.

The literature on alcohol abuse and inhalant and drug use by American Indian youth is reviewed here.   Work among Sioux populations is discussed as well as research on other Plains Indian groups.   Factors contributing to alcohol use by the very young are outlined, including parental tolerance of adolescent substance abuse, a belief in self-determination and individual autonomy, and the use of altered states of consciousness within the culture. The relationship between alcohol use and suicide among the Arapaho and Shoshone is reviewed.   Patterns of alcohol use and abuse are explored, along with what are thought to be the reasons for the behavior.   Currently, beer drinking predominates and is disproportionately higher among American Indian young people than among Anglo-Americans or any other ethnic minority youth group.   Young American Indians also use inhalants and marijuana at disproportionately higher rates than other American youth.   The cultural matrix, which either worsens or retards drug use, is discussed.   Included in that matrix are such factors as peer group encouragement, laissez-faire child-rearing practices, conflicts between cultural ideals and behavioral realities, parental and community attitudes about drug use, and existing adult drug use models.   It is concluded that the ramifications of drug abuse and its endemic quality in the American Indian culture are such as to require societal interventions in the economic, attitudinal, educational, familial, and cultural areas. 79 Ref.

Weibel-Orlando, J.   "Substance Abuse Among American Indian Youth: A Continuing Crisis,"   Journal of Drug Issues, 14(2), pp. 313-335, 1984.

Supported by G-2-R01-AA04817-03 NIAAA and the California State Department of Alcohol and Drug Programs, administered by the UCLA Alcohol Research Center.   The literature on alcohol abuse and inhalant and drug use by American Indian youth is reviewed. Work among Sioux populations is discussed, as well as research on other Plains Indian groups.   Factors contributing to alcohol use by the very young are outlined, including parental tolerance of adolescent substance abuse, a belief in self-determination and individual autonomy, and the use of altered states of consciousness within the culture.   The relationship between alcohol use and suicide among the Arapaho and

Shoshone is reviewed. Patterns of alcohol use and abuse are explored, along with what are thought to be the reasons for the behavior. It is stated that currently, beer drinking predominates and is disproportionately higher among American Indian young people that among Anglo-Americans or any other ethnic minority youth group. Young American Indians also use inhalants and marijuana at disproportionately higher rates than other American youth. The cultural matrix, which either worsens or retards drug use, is discussed. Included in that matrix are such factors as peer group encouragement, laissez-faire child-rearing practices, conflicts between cultural ideals and behavioral realities, parental and community attitudes about drug use, and existing adult drug use models. It is concluded that the ramifications of drug abuse and its endemic quality in American Indian culture are such as to require societal interventions in the economic, attitudinal, educational, familial, and cultural areas.

Weidman, A. "Compulsive Adolescent Substance Abuser: Psychological Differentiation and Family Process," Journal of Drug Education, 13(2): 161-172, 1983.

The relationship was studied between psychological differentiation and locus of control among compulsive adolescent substance abusers who are residents of a therapeutic community and their parents. It was found that compulsive adolescent substance abusers are psychologically undifferentiated. These adolescents are involved in a pseudo-individuated relationship with their mothers who are psychologically and emotionally unavailable while their fathers are peripheral. The findings that these adolescents become more undifferentiated and maintain more internal locus of control beliefs as time in the program increases are attributed to the effects of residence in a therapeutic community. The residents internalize the therapeutic community belief system of personal responsibility while substituting dependence on their mothers and on alcohol and other drugs for dependence on the therapeutic community. Implications for treatment are discussed. 28 Ref.

Westermeyer, Joseph; Neider, John. "Cultural Affiliation Among American Indian Alcoholics: Correlations and Change Over a Ten Year Period," Journal of Operational Psychiatry. 1985, vol. 16(2) 17-23.

Whittaker, J. O. "Alcohol and the Standing Rock Sioux Tribe; a Twenty-year Follow-up Study," Journal of Studies on Alcohol, 43: 191-200, 1982.

In an interesting 20-year follow-up study of alcohol use among reservation Standing Rock Sioux, interviews were conducted in 1980 with 184 subjects (109 women) at least 12 years of age lowered from 15 in 1960).   In 1960, 31 percent of the sample abstained, 45 percent drank occasionally, and 24 percent drank regularly; the figures for 1980 were 42 percent (29 percent of the men and 50 percent of the women), 27 percent (20 percent of the men and 32 percent of the women), and 31 percent (50 percent of the men and 17 percent of the women), respectively. Of the drinkers 40 percent of the men and 16 of the women considered themselves alcoholics, and of the nondrinkers, 50 percent of the men and 18 percent of the women considered themselves recovering alcoholics. It is estimated that 16 percent of the population over 12 years of age is alcoholic--5 times more than in the U. S. non-Indian population and the highest of any ethnic group.   In 1960, 56 percent of the drinkers consumed an average of 1-2 bottles of beer, glasses of wine or drinks of distilled spirits per occasion, whereas 64 percent in 1980 did and only 4 percent of a comparison group of Whites did.   An estimated 50 percent of men and 25 percent of women over 40 were alcoholics.   There were more young women and juvenile drinkers in 1980.   Drug use, which was unknown in 1960, was found in 39 percent of the drinkers and is a problem primarily among juveniles, especially males. The number of classic symptoms of alcoholism increased greatly over the 20 years to equal that of non-Indians, the only major difference being that Indians almost never drink alone.

Wingert, J. L.   "Inhalant Use Among Native American Adolescents: A Comparison of Users and Nonusers At Intermountain Intertribal School,"   Dissertation. Dissertation Abstracts, Part B. 44; 2; 620B, 1983.

The purpose of this study was to compare a non-inhalant group of students (control group) with a group of inhalant users.   There were 20 nonusers, 21 repeat users and 21 onetime users, all of whom were personally interviewed,   and administered a questionnaire with 11 research variables to answer.   School records and importance of group membership for each student was looked at.   Significant differences between the two groups showed up on 6 of 11 research variables;   significant differences also showed up between the nonuser and repeat user group.   Recommendations include the necessity of early intervention, treatment, possibility of preventive programs, and implications for research.

Young, T.K.   "Self-perceived and Clinically Assessed Health Status: Analysis of a Health Survey," Canadian Journal of Public Health. 73(4):   273-277, 1982.

Results of a community health survey among Indian residents in region of isolated settlements in Ontario are reported. Prevalence rates for certain health problems, including excessive alcohol intake, were established, and the discrepancy between perceived and clinically determined health status was highlighted. 11 Ref.

9

SUICIDE

Berman, Alan L. "Socio-Cultural Autopsy: Self-Destructive Behavior Among The Duck Valley Indians," Conference paper. 12th Annual Meeting of the American Association of Suicidology, Denver, CO.: May 1979. 65 ABS.

Six-Duck Valley is a suicidogenic Community. Situated 140 miles southeast of Boise, Idaho, and 100 miles from the nearest population center of over 6,000, this reservation of roughly 1,000 Shoshone and Paiute Indians is both isolated and depressed. The political, economic, and social factors which influence the reservation's isolation and depression are discussed. The number one public health problem at Duck Valley is alcoholism. Getting drunk is pervasive and socially sanctioned, especially among the young. Of all arrests made, 75 percent are alcohol related; one-half of these are arrests for driving or riding in a moving vehicle. There is no organized and supported initiative to provide programmatic intervention. No detoxification center is available; and the Indian Health Service Hospital maintains a closed-door policy toward alcoholics, preferring to merely transfer them to the drunk tank to sober up. Two of four 1977 suicides took place in the drunk tank. Overall, 86 percent of completed suicides at Duck Valley are alcohol related. The author concludes that suicidal behavior at Duck Valley most often occurs as an unplanned and impulsive act. It is an indirect statement of pain, despair, or revenge by a youth laden with helplessness. 11 Ref.

Blackwood, Larry Health Problems of the Alaska Natives: Suicide Mortality and Morbidity. Rockville, Md.: Indian Health Service, 1978, 19 p.

The purpose of this study is to present information concerning suicide mortality and morbidity in the state of Alaska. The study is divided into five sections and includes such information as the 1951-1975 trend, Age-specific and age-adjusted rates, sex differences, suicide methods, service unit differences, total reported morbidity, age distribution, sex distribution, role of alcohol, service unit differences in morbidity, and seasonal variations. In order to determine such information, sources included vital statistics from the Indian Health Service by the national Center for Health Statistics. Mortality figures were reported by Kraus (N.D.), morbidity data from IHS inpatient/outpatient reporting system reports, and statistic reports from The National Center for Health Statistics and from the Bureau of Census. DAR

Fox, J., Manitowabi, D., Ward, J.A. "Indian Community with a High Suicide Rate: 5 years After," Canadian Journal of Psychiatry 29(5): 425-427, 1984.

The results of a five-year follow-up study concerning a suicide epidemic on a Manitoulin Island Indian Reserve in 1974 and 1975 are reported here. In the succeeding years, the suicide rate had dropped to a tenth of the level of the epidemic and has reached the levels for the rest of Manitoulin Island, including the white and Native Indian population. There has been a corresponding drop in the rate of violent death and of the number of suicide attempts. It is suggested here that the following programs and activities, which included multidimensional prevention and intervention measures, have contributed to the improvement: (1) in addition to a conventional residential alcohol recovery program, the Rainbow Lodge Recovery Center used family outreach programs with the inclusion of family members in the alcohol group process; (2) the program organized nonalcoholic community feasts with different presentations of entertainment and tradition; (3) the program helped youth to gain stature by enabling them to provide services to the community; (4) in the schools, alcohol counselors presented a program of self-esteem enhancement, promotion of traditional values, and alcohol education; and (5) health nurses, local general practitioners, two Native mental health workers, and the traveling mental health team with the backup institution were part of an organized intervention approach. 9 Ref.

Grove, O.; Lynge, J. "Suicide and Attempted Suicide in Greenland. A Controlled Study in Nuuk (Godthaab)," Acta-Psychiatr-Scand. 1979 Oct. 60 (4). p 375-91.

Suicidal behavior in Eskimo populations has changed in pattern and quantity over the last decades. Rates have more than quadrupled and performers now are mainly

young persons with obscure motivation. In a study from
Greenland's major township all cases of attempted or
completed suicide among Greenlanders are analyzed for
social,   emotional,   somatic,   and   environmental
predisposing factors in comparison with a non-
psychiatric, never-suicidal, matching group. Almost
two per thousand of the adult population committed
suicide yearly whole attempts at suicide were five
times as frequent. A quarrelsome, drinking, childhood
home background was often found, at least as regards
the attempters, who themselves frequently suffered from
emotional conflicts with close contacts, alcohol
affliction, criminality, and instability at work.
Neither bereavement, cross-cultural exposure, broken
homes, nor meteorological factors seem to exert a
significant influence. The results are discussed in
relation to the social and cultural evolution of the
Greenlandic society. Author.

Miller, Marv. "Suicides on a Southwestern American
Indian Reservation," White Cloud Journal, vol. (3) p.
14-18, 1979.

Results showed suicides clustered by day of the week,
season, and reservation location, and typical victims
as young unmarried males holding unskilled or
semiskilled jobs. Suggested are strategies maximizing
suicide prevention efforts.

Shore, James H. "Suicide and Suicide Attempts Among
American Indians of the Pacific Northwest," The
International Journal of Social Psychiatry, 1972, 18,
2, Sum., 91-96.

Suicide and suicide attempt behavior among American
Indians of the Pacific Northwest was studied over a
one-year period from data gathered by mental health
field personnel using a structured suicidology form.
The service population included reservation Indians
from nine major Northwest tribes and an Indian boarding
school. The purpose was to make tribal comparisons of
the pattern of self-destructive behavior, to develop a
program of crisis intervention and suicide prevention,
and to establish a reliable statistical data base. The
annual completed suicide rate for the total Indian
population was 28 per 100,000. A high ratio of suicide
attempts to completed suicides was discovered: 16 to
1. The profile of the completed suicide subject was
that of an Indian man in his 30's, single or separated,
who hung or shot himself. This contrasted with the
profile of the suicide attempt subject who was
typically a young Indian female ingesting drugs. The
suicide attempt took place at home, precipitated by a
quarrel with a relative or friend with the intent to

change a relationship or express anger. An attempt was often associated with the use of alcohol and discovered by direct communication with another person. Thirty attempts took place at the Indian boarding school. Adolescent girls composed 92 percent of these attempts with a significant over-representation of Northwest students in the suicide attempt group. This appeared to be related to a differential policy of boarding school referral, selecting high risk students form the Pacific Northwest region. Suicide and suicide attempt epidemics occur in which a major ethiologic factor is a learned pattern of self-destructive behavior with an extended family or peer group. In certain communities this occurs in a particular physical setting and is strongly influenced by cultural factors.

Spaulding, John M. Recent Suicide Rates Among Ten Ojibwa Indian Bands in Northwestern Ontario," Omega, 1985-1986, 16, 4, 347-354.

This study was designed to investigate the rate of completed suicides for ten Ojibwa Indian Bands in Northwestern Ontario for the years 1975 to 1982. Records from medical services, health and welfare Canada (1), were reviewed for suicide date and individual interviews were conducted with nine Native health workers to corroborate these data. Results indicated an overall rate of 61.7 suicides per 100,000 population. Suicide victims tended to be young males who used firearms as a method. Alcohol or drug use was directly involved in over half of the suicides.

Starkey, P.; Santora, D. "Research Studies in American Indian Suicides," Journal of Psychiatric Nursing and Mental Health Services. 20(8): 25-29, 1982.

Research literature is reviewed concerning suicides within Indian tribes in the southwestern and northwestern regions of the United States. It is noted that alcohol use and abuse has been found to be involved in a majority of these suicides. Further research is needed to identify tribal-specific variables in relation to suicidal behavior, since it is difficult to generalize about suicide patterns among the 493 diverse American Indian tribes. Such research would generate data on the characteristics of individuals considered to be at high risk for suicide within a specific tribe, and would aid in the delivery of culturally-relevant mental health care. 21 Ref.

United States. Department of Health Education and Welfare. National Institute of Mental Health. Center for Studies of Crime and Delinquency. Suicide, Homicide and Alcoholism Among American Indians:

Guidelines for Help. by Calvin Frederick and others.
Washington, D.C.:Government Printing Office, 1973.

This manual is the result of a series of workshops
developed in response to a request by the BIA for
material to equip criminal justice personnel to deal
more effectively with problems of suicidal behavior and
alcoholism among young American Indians, and is offered
for professionals and nonprofessionals who wish to work
in the area of crisis intervention. Ten preventative
steps for dealing with the suicidal patient are: 1)
Listen. 2) Evaluate the seriousness of the patients
thoughts and feelings. 3) Evaluate the intensity or
severity of the emotional disturbance. 4) Take every
complaint and feeling the patient expresses seriously.
5) Do not be afraid to ask directly if the individual
has entertained thoughts of suicide. 6) Do not be
misled by the person's comments that he is alright and
past the crisis. 7) Be affirmative but supportive. 8)
Evaluate the resources available, both inner
psychological resources and outer resources in his
environment. 9) Act specifically by doing something
tangible. 10) Do not be afraid to ask for assistance
and consultation. Additional techniques include
providing a safe and provocative free environment,
assurance that his depression is temporary, pointing
out the finality of suicide, and avoidance of
negativitism in the helper/patient interaction.
Ingredients of a prevention program are given: basic
community support beginning with the tribal council, 24
hour service, use of Indian counselors, involvement of
law enforcement officers, assistance in housing and
employment needs, and creation of voc-rehab centers for
high risk communities. Safe-proofing of jails is
stressed with preventive procedures to be taken.
Removal of personal items and bedding that might be
used to commit suicide. Guards should be primary
intervention staff with consultation. Intoxicated
persons should be held in special quarters, and
medications should be controlled by those in charge.
While the physical and psychological environment is
important, nothing takes the place of personal contact
and understanding in time of crisis. An extensive
background is given with causes for suicide, homicide,
and alcoholism. Contains 7 tables of death rates
including alcohol related; two appendixes containing
population data from the 1960 and '70 censuses and a
list of Community Mental Health Programs serving
Indians and Alaska natives. 29 references.

10

TREATMENT

Bain, D., and Taylor, L. Counseling Skills for Alcoholism Treatment Services: A Literature Review and Experience Survey, Toronto, Ontario, Canada: Health and Welfare Canada, 1979.

The present study was conducted in response to an absence of organized knowledge concerning the identification and assessment of existing therapeutic counseling skills relevant to the treatment of alcohol abusers. In pursuit of this knowledge, the following questions were explored: (1) Which treatment approaches are frequently used with alcoholics and what counseling skills facilitate their effectiveness? (2) What are the unique needs of special client populations, and which counseling skills are particularly important in meeting these needs?, and (3) To what extent do alcoholism counselors require unique skills? Three principal sources are used to explore these questions: research-based conclusions from the literature, theoretical bases that were applied in the literature, and the clinical knowledge of selected individuals experienced in training and evaluating alcoholism treatment counselors and their skills. The more salient and pertinent observations which arose from this study are presented. Native peoples and youth are discussed in this volume. 256 Ref.

Beiser, M.; Attneave, C.L. "Mental Disorders Among Native American Children: Rates and Risk Periods for Entering Treatment," American Journal of Psychiatry. 139(2): 193-198, 1982.

National data on the use of outpatient mental health services by Native American children in 1974 are compared with 1969 national data on non-Indian children. It was found that, at all ages except five to nine years, Indian children were at higher risk for entering the treatment system than were non-Indian children, and that utilization patterns varied by age and sex. Alcohol misuse as an antisocial behavior problem among Indian teenagers between 15 and 19 years old was evident. Possible reasons for these high risk rates demonstrated by Indian children are discussed, including implications for further studies. 30 Ref.

Berg, Lawrence, et al. "Patient Care and Health Provider Attitudes in Alaska," Journal of Social Psychiatry. 1978, vol 24(4) 276-280.

One hundred forty community health aides in Alaskan villages (half of the total number) responded to a mailed questionnaire, the opinions about mental illness (OMI) scale, which was also administered to all the other health providers (at all levels) in the state (in twelve medical facilities and twenty alcohol programs). Data were grouped with respect to geographic location, occupation, and agency type (medical to geographic location, occupation, and agency type (medical facility or alcoholism program). Anovas were used to test independently the main effect of geographic area, occupation, and type of agency for each profile factor. No consistent pattern was seen in the professional scores within areas. A high degree of negative association was found between authoritarianism and social restrictiveness and the amount of academic training. mental hygiene ideology (high treatment orientation and humanitarian perspective) tended to be positively associated with academic training. Alcoholism treatment agencies scored significantly higher on benevolence and mental hygiene ideology scales. The question is raised as to whether or not these results can be used as screening devices for choice of personnel to work with consumers, but caution is urged about applying the results without outcome studies. (11 Ref.).

Blum, Kenneth; Futterman, Sanford, L.; Pascorosa, Paul "Peyote, A Potential Ethnopharmocologic Agent for Alcoholism and Other Drug Dependencies: Possible Biochemical Rationale," Clinical Toxicology 1977 vol 11(4) 459-472.

Examines Folk Psychiatry among Native American church members from an ethnopharmacologic viewpoint. Alcohol and opiate abuse among Indians and non-Indians are presented in three case histories proving to be asymptomatic under Indian guidance and through participation in the peyote ritual. The biochemical alkaloids common in the peyote cactus, rather than just the psychoactive substances (mescaline), are purported to be pharmacologically similar to the neuroaminederived alkaloids found in the brain during alcohol intoxication. Evidence is reviewed that points out possible common features of alcohol and opiate dependence, leading to the speculation that a common mode of treatment may reside in plants rich in isoquinoline alkaloids. (63 Ref.).

Brown, L. "Introduction to Program Planning and Evaluation of Native Alcohol Programs," Conference paper. 2nd Annual meeting of the Special Interest Group on Program Evaluation, Canadian Addiction Foundation. Regina, Canada: 8-9 Sep. 1982. 184 p. (pp. 157-184).

Evaluation does not have to be a frightening or even threatening event for a native (Canadian Indian) alcohol program if evaluation is understood and used as part of the program on a daily basis, i.e., the method by which Native programs are to be evaluated should be created by Native people as part of the original planning process of the program. A procedure for planning and evaluating Native alcohol treatment programs is outlined. This method is based on and compatible with the program planning model of the Nechi Training Institute (Canada), which is designed to train individuals from the native community in alcoholism counseling. 8 Ref.

Burns, Thomas R. "A Survey of Attitudes Toward Alcoholics and Alcohol Programs Among Indian Health Service Personnel," White Cloud Journal. 1981 vol. 2(3) 25-30.

Surveyed fifty health professionals in the Phoenix area of the U.S. Indian Health Service to find out their attitudes toward American Indian Alcoholics and their service unit's alcoholism treatment program. SS completed a five-page questionnaire which showed that, as a group, they felt slightly positive about their program and slightly less positive about their clients. Results were correlated across the professions of physician, social worker, and nurse. (7 Ref.).

Callahan, K.L. Ph.D. Dissertation, Purdue University, 1981.

This study proposed to conduct an ethnographic needs assessment of Papago Indian alcohol-abusers and alcoholics, a population for whom extensive problem drinking has been well documented. By using methods of ethnography and needs assessment studies the following goals were sought: the documentation of the sociodemographic characteristics of Papago problem drinkers, the documentation of their drinking patterns, the documentation of the kinds of intervention strategies available to them, an exploration of the network of relationships operant among the interventions, an investigation into the Papago view and opinion of the interventions, and the establishment of Papago needs. Data was collected by examining client records, interviews with a sample population of Papago urban problem drinkers, and interviews with staff members of interventions. It was then assessed on the basis of knowledge gained through observation within the system of intervention strategies. The data revealed that there was no statistically significant difference between the Papago drinking population and the general Papago population in terms of sociodemographics. The Papago learn normative drinking behavior at an early age and excessive drinking behavior often appears during the teen years. Papago drinking styles include the acute public drunk, the periodic alcohol-abuser, the consistent alcohol abuser, and the alcoholic; these styles are what is termed abnormal or problem drinking. Papago drinking is a social activity which reinforces social acceptance and facilitates social interaction and cohesion. There is an extensive system of intervention strategies available to Papago problem drinkers but many programs are Anglo-oriented--unresponsive to problems specific to Papago drinkers. This system is not extensively utilized by the Papago; and therefore, they are not receiving a comprehensive system of care. There are ways in which existing services can be redesigned and this together with the implementation of new services will provide for a comprehensive system of care targeted to the Papago. The most pressing need of the Papago is the implementation of education and prevention programs.

Colorado, P. "Traditional Values and Culture in Treatment," Conference paper. 1981 Annual School on Alcohol and Addiction Studies, Anchorage, AK.: 4-7, May, 1981. 345 p. (pp. 267-313).

A theoretical framework of traditional Native American treatment is presented. The present conditions in the field of Native alcoholism and the historical use of alcohol by Native Americans are described, including what has been done in this field by professionals, by Native Americans on their own, and by western scientists. It is contended that alcohol was uniquely suited as a tool of expropriation, and that traditional Native American systems of medicine, which could have softened the assault of alcoholism, were deliberately destroyed by European settlers. A new theoretical approach to Native American alcoholism, called "invasion reaction," is presented. This approach recognizes the history of Native people and the physical, sociocultural, emotional, and spiritual aspects of Native life. Comments and questions by workshop participants are addressed.

Curran, J. "West German Therapy May Be Used to Treat Maine Indians," Bangor Daily News. Bangor, ME: 14, July, 1982.

It is reported that an alcohol abuse program for Native Americans in Maine may include the Good Templar Society Program, which provides alcoholism treatment for four Maine Indians at a West German clinic. The project is designed to integrate and develop educational, preventive, and treatment programs to meet the cultural needs of Native Americans. German interest in American Indians reportedly grew as a result of the environmentalist and peace movements, and as a result of the perspective on environmental issues offered by American Indians.

D'Arcy, C.; Fritz, W. "Comparisons: Indian and Non-Indian Use of Psychiatric Services," Canadian Journal of Psychiatry. 27(3): 194-203, 1982.

Results are presented from a study designed to examine the major differences between the Saskatchewan (Canada) Indian and non-Indian population in regard to the prevalence of psychiatric disorders, rates of treatment, and the mix of inpatient and outpatient services they receive. It was found that: (1) diagnostic and treatment differences between these two populations were more pronounced in the "private" than in the "public" treatment sector; and (2) the largest relative differences between populations were in the prevalence of mental retardation, followed by psychoses, neuroses, and alcoholism. These findings are discussed in relation to demographic, socioeconomic and cultural differences, and to size and organizational differences between the "public and "private" treatment sectors. 21 Ref.

Dominick, George P. "Community Programs for the Treatment of Alcoholics," In: Ralph E. Tarter and Arthur A. Sugerman, (eds.) Alcoholism, Reading, MA: Addison-Wesley, 1976, 857 p. (pp. 777-834).

A discussion is presented on community programs which are those programs providing services to persons without respect to creed, color, or the ability to pay, and are carried out by Federal, State, County, or Local groups. The author draws upon personal experience as a member of a multidisciplinary team in Georgia which established community treatment programs. He presents eight basic assumptions upon which a treatment philosophy can be based. Problems encountered at the level of administrative planning are considered. Components of comprehensive services, such as an emergency care system and inpatient care, are discussed in terms of the treatment process. Programs for youth, the elderly, and American Indians are briefly described. Important aspects of outreach, education, and prevention programs are mentioned. 64 Ref.

Ferguson, L.D. Indian Clients Treated in NIAAA-Funded Programs: Calendar Year 1980. Rockville, Md.: National Institute on Alcohol Abuse and Alcoholism, 1981, 16 p.

Data are reviewed concerning American Indian clients treated in programs funded by the national Institute on Alcohol Abuse and Alcoholism (NIAAA) during calendar year 1980. Clients in programs specifically funded to treat Indians are compared to Indian clients in all other categorical programs.

Flores, P.J. "Alcoholism Treatment and the Relationship of Native American Cultural Values to Recovery," Dissertation, University of Arizona, Tucson, Arizona. 1983.

Native American groups have been reported to suffer disproportionately higher rates of alcohol-related disorders than does the dominant Anglo population. This problematic situation is compounded by the fact that Native Americans have a far lower rate of alcoholism recovery than do most other groups receiving treatment. Research recommendations underscore the necessity of matching the philosophy and methods of a treatment program to fit the specific cultural values of Native American alcoholics. To test this hypothesis, a study was conducted to provide empirical and descriptive data that would help determine if specific value differences between Anglos and Native Americans could be identified. Subjects were 34 male and 9 female Native Americans who were voluntary admissions into an inpatient treatment program in a southwestern community mental health center over a nine month period (1981 to 1982) and Anglo staff at this treatment center. It was found that Native Americans do have poorer prognosis rates of alcoholism recovery, and that values of Native Americans are measurable and significantly different from values of Anglos. The claim that cultural influences override individual pathology and personality differences was not supported, indicating that alcohol overrides cultural influences and differences. Native Americans proved to be more similar to other alcoholics (even if these alcoholics were Anglo) than they were to the nonalcoholic cultural peers when value differences on the Rokeach Value Survey were excluded from comparisons.

Flores, P.J.   "Alcoholism Treatment and the Relationship of Native American Cultural Values to Recovery," International Journal of the Addictions. 1985-1986, vol. 20(11-12) 1707-1726.

Grinspoon, L.; Bakalar, J.B.   "Psychedelic Drug Therapies,"   In: J.H. Masserman, ed., Current Psychiatric Therapies: Vol. 20 -1981. New York, NY: Grune & Stratton, 1981. 416 p. (pp. 275-283).

It is reported that lysergic acid diethylamide (LSD) often produces powerful immediate effects on alcoholics; however, the question is whether these effects can be readily translated into enduring change. Findings from earlier studies have indicated that about 50 percent of severe chronic alcoholics treated with a single dose of LSD recovered and were sober a year or two later.   It is noted that these earlier studies had insufficient controls, and most lacked objective measures of change, adequate follow-up, and other safeguards; consequently, more carefully designed research have not produced consistently promising results with LSD treatment.   It is contended, however, that it would be wrong to conclude that psychedelic experience can never be a turning point in the life of an alcoholic, e.g., Bill Wilson, founder of Alcoholics Anonymous, equates his LSD trip to a sudden religious illumination that changed his life.   The use of mescaline in the form of peyote by Native Americans is regarded as, among other things, part of a treatment of alcoholism, i.e., it is believed that those who participate in the peyote ritual are more likely to be abstinent.

Hall, R.L.   "Alcohol Treatment in American-Indian Populations - An Indigenour Treatment Modality Compared with Traditional Approaches," Annals of the New York Academy of Sciences. vol. 472, July, 1986, 168-178.

Hedin, C.   Statistical Report on Albuquerque Area Alcoholism Treatment Program Activities and an Overview of the Problems Related to Indian Substance Abuse. Indian Health Service, Preventive Health Programs Branch, Albuquerque, NM: 1981, 29 p.

Data are presented concerning alcoholism treatment programs and services for the Native American community in the Albuquerque (New Mexico) area during FY 1982. These data were derived from the Annual Alcoholism

Treatment Guidance System (ATGS) report for FY 1982. Some comparisons are drawn between the Native American Project Information System (NAPIS) and ATGS to reveal any indications of trends over the past five years, between 1978 and 1982. Additional data are included to assemble an apparent interrelationship between alcohol abuse and other Indian community characteristics. Information is provided on (1) referral patterns and sources; (2) client activity and characteristics; (3) program activity and accomplishments; (4) client characteristics at discharge from treatment; (5) alcohol-related accidents; (6) suicide rates and leading causes of death; and (7) tribal criminal offenses related to alcoholism and alcohol abuse. 10 Ref.

Hodgson, M. "Some Comments on Evaluation and Native Programs," Conference paper. 2nd Annual Meeting of the Special Interest Group on Program Evaluation, Canadian Addiction Foundation. Regina, Canada: 8-0 Sept., 1982. 184 p. (pp. 152-156).

The Nechi (Ojibwa term for "people") Training Institute in Alberta, Canada was designed to train sober alcoholics from the Indian community of Canada in alcoholism counseling. The development of Nechi is described to demonstrate how long it took to change the attitudes of the Native Canadian and research consultant communities about the need for program evaluation.

Hudson, C.J. "Agoraphobia in Alaskan Eskimo," New York State Journal of Medicine. 81(2): 224-225, 1981.

A case report of a 31-year-old Eskimo male with agoraphobia is presented. It has been reported that as many as one-third of the alcoholics in a series of patients were suffering from severe agoraphobia or other social phobias. Because it is possible that many Native Americans suffer from severe phobias such as agoraphobia, which is a potentially treatable cause of alcoholism it is suggested that all problem drinkers be screened for phobic symptoms. For Native Americans, this effort will require careful study, diligent work, and patient understanding of the cultural issues involved. 7 Ref.

Hurlburt, G.; Gade, E; Fuqua, F. "Intercorrelational Structure of the Eysenk Personality Questionnaire with an Alcoholic Population," Psychological Reports. 51(2): 515-520, 1982.

A heterogeneous group of 237 alcoholics who had just completed alcoholic detoxification treatment was administered the Eysenck Personality Questionnaire. The alcoholics scored higher than their appropriate normative groups on the dimensions of toughmindedness, emotionality, and the tendency to fake.   All the alcoholics groups scored lower on extroversion than their norm groups except Caucasian females.   All groups except Caucasian males tended to have higher lie scale than their norm groups.   Native American alcoholics had higher psychoticism and lie scores and lower extraversion scores than the Caucasian alcoholics.   Only the toughmindedness   and   emotionality   scales   were significantly related.   Results indicate that the questionnaire is appropriate for use with Native American alcoholics.   14 Ref.

Katz, P.   "Psychotherapy with Native Adolescents," Canadian Journal of Psychiatry,   26 (7):   455-459, 1981.

Examples of psychotherapy with Cree and Saulteaux-Ojibwa tribe natives are used to show that the therapist who wishes to treat adolescents from native cultures such as the Canadian Indian must learn about a different set of values, develop new communication skills and reexamine many standard practices.   One case is reviewed where a 15-year-old Saulteaux-Ojibwa boy whose parents were alcoholic and had separated when he was very young had begun to emulate his siblings in their path toward alcohol abuse and delinquent behavior.   6 Ref.

Kunitz, S.J.; Levy, J.E.   "Economic and Political Factors Inhibiting the Use of Basic Research Findings in Indian Alcoholism Programs,"   Journal of Studies on Alcohol.   Suppl. No. 9:60-72, 1981.

Some of the political, ideological, and economic characteristics of American Indian alcoholism treatment programs are examined, which tend to inhibit the utilization of research findings, specifically, in a time of fiscal constriction.   Using examples of research findings on Indian drinking, it is argued that such findings will be rejected by treatment programs if they do not coincide with prevalent treatment ideologies, or if they are perceived as threatening the major   economic   function   of   these   programs. Considerably more basic as well as innovative evaluation research is necessary among Indian populations, if an adequate understanding of the nature of Indian drinking and the development of effective treatment programs are to be achieved.   13 Ref.

Merker, J. F.   "Indians of the Great Plains: Issues in Counseling and Family Therapy,"   Conference paper, New

Orleans, LA: 13 April 1981. 9 p.

It is contended that the Indians of the Great Plains, primarily the Omaha, Winnebago, and Sioux, challenge the 1980's with significant problems in alcoholism. Problems encountered in counseling and treating these Native Americans are discussed. Methods and approaches used by the Lincoln (Nebraska) Indian Center and the Lincoln Veterans Administration Medical Center to circumvent these problems are described.

Merrill, Orville William, Jr.   "Group Psychotherapy with American Indian Adolescents: A Study of Reported Changes," Ph.D. Dissertation, 1974. Dissertation Abstracts International, 35/03-B, 1932.

Considered here were seven questions pertaining to group psychotherapy with American Indian adolescents. Each topic was examined and measured in order to answer seven questions comprising the problem of the study. The importance of the study derives from research showing the mental health needs of American Indians in general, and for preventive and treatment programs for American Indian students in boarding schools. The data were obtained from pre and post-therapy ratings of attitudes, feelings, and behavior of the subjects. Reporting sources were the subjects and school personnel. The fifty-six hypotheses referred to the subjects significantly increasing in these variables: Self-understanding, self-concept, self-confidence, verbal expression, good behavior at school, and good relationships with others. A comparison of self-reported changes by the subjects and control group subjects indicated: Control group subjects reported significant decrease in physically expressing anger. The consistent subjects reported significant increases in self-respect and self-confidence in classes. A significant decrease was reported in solvent sniffing. Consistent subjects compared to inconsistent subjects reported significant increases in these areas: Self-understanding, good verbal expression, self-respect, self-confidence in classes, and good interpersonal relationships. Significant decreases were reported in the following: Depression, anxiety, physical problems, and physically expressing anger. School personnel reported that subjects increased in these areas: Self-expression in classes, self confidence, and getting angry at others. Decreases were reported in sleeping well at night, good relationships with reporting teachers, and good relationships with students. It was concluded that group therapy is an effective treatment modality for American Indian adolescents.

Nighhswander, T.S. " High Utilizers of Ambulatory Care
Services: 6-year Follow-up at Alaska Native Medical
Center," Public Health Reports. 99(4):   400-404,
1984.

A study was conducted to investigate who uses
ambulatory care services most, what their problems are,
and what happens to them over time. Subjects were a
random sample of 100 chosen from the 698 patients who
visited the Alaska Native Medical Center 15 times or
more in 1972. The center's primary clientele consists
of Indians, Aleuts, and Eskimos living in south central
Alaska. Of the 100 subjects, 78 were women and 22 were
men. The retrospective study followed them for the 6
years between 1973 and 1978. Subjects were matched by
age and sex with a control patient who had visited the
center three times or less in the same period. The
high-utilizer group contained substantially more women
than men in all age groups. The same relationship
existed in the general clinic population in all age
groups but one--those born in the 1970s' where males
predominated slightly. In general, high-utilizer men
were older than high-utilizer women. During follow-up,
the men in the high-utilizer group had three times the
number of hospitalizations as the controls, and the
women had twice the number of admissions. At the end
of the follow-up, 1 of every 4 men of the high-utilizer
group had died; of the women, 1 of every 10 had died.
Half of these deaths were associated with alcohol. It
is concluded that several approaches to high-utilizer
patients are useful. A well-organized medical record,
with a complete problem list and index, is considered
imperative. Recommended as helpful, too, is having
only one or several health care providers consistently
see the patient at each visit. The findings indicate
that high utilizers must be recognized as a subgroup at
high risk for hospitalization and early death. 6 Ref.

Orford, J. "Prevention and Management of Alcohol
Problems in the Family Setting: A Review of Work
Carried Out in English-speaking Countries" Alcohol and
Alcoholism, 19(2): 109-122, 1984.

A review of studies on alcoholism treatment and the
family is presented and the issues as they pertain to
non-English-speaking countries are discussed...there
are at least six theoretical perspectives on alcohol
misuse and the family: the disturbed personality
perspective, the stress victim perspective, the systems
perspective, the cultural patterning perspective, the
ecological perspective, and the contagion perspective.
Adherence to one or to a limited range of viewpoints
inhibits the effectiveness of clinicians. Treatment of
alcohol problems in the family setting is effective

often before the problems are unmanageable. Nonspecialist professional agencies who encounter family problems often fail to identify or deal with alcohol misuse when it is present. Trained voluntary workers may be effective in the treatment of alcohol problems within the family context. It was concluded that alcohol misuse should not be dealt with separately from other health and social problems. 95 Ref.

Query, J. M. "Comparative Admission and Follow-up Study of American Indians and Whites in a Youth Chemical Dependency Unit on the North Central Plains," International Journal of the Addictions, 20(3): 489-502, 1985.

This study focused on drug abusing young adults in North Dakota. Nonrural youth were more likely to be in a state treatment program than rural youth. Few etiological differences between white and Indian youth existed, although Indian youth were over represented tenfold. They could be described as young people in trouble at school and with the law, who were sexually involved but not religiously so. In a six-month follow-up study, positive outcome data were much stronger for white than Indian patients, raising seminal questions about the effectiveness of such programs for the Indian patient.

Rhodes, E.R.; Marshall, M.; Attneave, C.; et al. "Mental Health Problems of American Indians Seen in Outpatient Facilities of the Indian Health Service," Public Health Reports, (95) 4, 1975, 329-335.

The study here was undertaken to analyze patterns of mental health conditions as reflected in visits to outpatient care facilities of the Indian Health Service (IHS). Quantitative information about the mental health of American Indians obviously must come form the IHS. Diagnoses made in IHS clinics and hospitals are entered into a computer for subsequent tabulation and analysis; these diagnoses are classified as 'problems' or 'clinical impressions'. In addition problem checklists completed in the mental health or social services branches of IHS also provide useful information about Indians' reasons for seeking care. Data for this study were obtained from the office of program statistics of IHS. These data are contained in computer printouts showing the number of visits for various problems to IHS and contract facilities. Using these data, we constructed tables to compare the numbers and rates of visits for various diagnoses between different age groups for fiscal year 1975. The authors also similarly analyzed certain data relating to visits for mental health branches. The IHS lists the following conditions under the heading 'Mental disorders' for clinic visits: alcoholism, organic brain syndrome, schizophrenia and other psychoses, neurosis, personality disorders, and drug abuse and dependence. The IHS has 49 hospitals, 101 health centers, and more than 300 health stations. All of these facilities contribute reports to the computer center during the Fiscal year 1975, a total of 2,759,000 outpatient visits were made, and 58,637 (2.1%) of these visits were for mental disorders.

Rozynko, Vitali; Ferguson, Lara, C. "Admission Characteristics of Indian and White Alcoholic Patients in a Rural Mental Hospital," International Journal of the Addictions 1978 vol 13(4) 591-604.

Fifty-eight American Indian alcoholic admissions and two-hundred and eleven white alcoholic admissions to a California state mental hospital were interviewed utilizing a 141-item interview scale. The two groups were compared as to their responses to the interview items by a series of one-way anovas. Statistically significant differences were found on demographic, socioeconomic, hospitalization, drinking and friendship pattern variables. Results are discussed with reference to data reliability and socioeconomic and cultural factors. The study's findings are also related to an apparent need for the education of police and Native Americans in the area concerning treatment resources available to Native American problem drinkers. (14 Ref.)

Sanders, J.M. "Adolescents and Substance Abuse," Pediatrics 76(4): 630-632, 1985.

The American Academy of Pediatrics impaneled a Task Force with a specific Directive to advise the Executive Board on the most effective and reasonable activities the Academy should take against substance abuse. The Task Force recommendations included: (1) that pediatricians be educated on how to interview, identify, and counsel/manage young people and their families in medical school, during residency, and on a continuing-education basis; and (2) the Academy and all pediatricians should become actively involved in education efforts directed toward children, young people, the family, and the community. Projects were suggested to meet these objectives and a new Task Force on Substance Abuse was established. 3 Ref.

Shore, James H. and Kofoed, Lial. "Community Intervention in the Treatment of Alcoholism," Alcoholism: Clinical and Experimental Research. 1984, March-April, vol 8(2) 151-159.

Reviews research related to five examples of alcoholism treatment delivery systems: driver diversion, the public inebriate, outpatient and social detoxification, alcohol treatment for Native Americans, and treatment of the Alcoholic physician. Public policy and community intervention initiatives are discussed, and the effectiveness of these programs is examined. A significant growth of program development is apparent in all areas except outpatient and social detoxification. However, research findings have been derived from the medical model of alcoholism, which may have contributed to ambiguous social attitudes and less effective public policy. Patient treatment and social policy as public health approaches to the treatment of alcoholism are discussed.

Smith-Peterson, C. "Substance Abuse Treatment and Cultural Diversity," In: G. Bennett, et al., eds., Substance Abuse: ... Perspectives. New York, NY: John Wiley & Sons, 1983. 453 p. (pp. 370-382) $24.95.

This chapter has been organized to address the frequent omission of cultural variables in the consideration of treatment approaches and prevention strategies. It is based on the belief that past failures to acknowledge important cultural and ethnic differences in substance abuse problems and patterns in the United States have perpetuated problems in stereotyping, misunderstanding, and program effectiveness. Accordingly, the patterns and specific characteristics of substance abuse and related problems are considered in ethnic populations, including black Americans, Native Americans, and Hispanics. While the focus is on alcohol use patterns within a cultural context, anthropologic and sociologic perspectives are considered, with many of these concepts applying to the cultural context of other types of substance use and abuse. Implications for substance abuse treatment are identified. 19 Ref.

United States. Alcohol, Drug Abuse, and Mental Health Administration. Youth Treatment Conference (9th: 1983 Oct. 31 - Nov. 1: Indianapolis, Ind.). Rockville, Md., 1984.

Waddell, J.O. "Cultural Relativity and Alcohol Use: Implications for Research and Treatment," Journal of Studies on Alcohol. Suppl. No. 9:19-28, 1981.

A brief appraisal of the concept of cultural relativity is provided, and how it has been established in anthropological research concerning alcohol use and misuse is discussed. A three-part position is described that calls for the gathering of research and treatment data with a pluralistic and open mind, the recognition of the primacy of enculturative experience in the determination of human behavior, and the understanding that treatment design and outcome must be relevant to the population being treated. Implications of cultural relativity for treatment of alcohol-related health problems in specific cultural situations are explored. 26 Ref.

Waddell, J.O. "Alcoholic Patient as an Ethnographic Domain: The Anthropologist's Role in the Therapeutic Process," Journal of Studies on Alcohol. 42(9): 846-854, 1981.

The possibility of a cooperative exchange of ideas and information between the counselor or therapist who works with the alcoholic patient and the ethnographer who works with an alcoholic informant is explored.   5 Ref.

Waite, B. J., Ludwig, M. J. Growing Concern: How to Provide Services for Children from Alcoholic Families, Rockville, Md.: National Institute on Alcohol Abuse and Alcoholism, 1983.

This is designed to aid caregivers in identifying, intervening with, treating and preventing further problems of children of alcoholic parents.   The National Institute on Alcohol Abuse and Alcoholism was involved here in sponsoring the development of resource materials on issues and service needs of this population.   The purpose of this publication is to provide caregivers with such information.   Problems and needs of children of alcoholics are outlined, and appropriate approaches for meeting these needs are described, including their role of caregivers. Organizational issues and the role of cultural issues in the provision of services to these children are discussed.   A reading list on children of alcoholics, and brief descriptions of programs reaching these children are appended.   102 Ref.

Westermeyer, Joseph; Neider, John   "Predicting Treatment Outcome After Ten Years Among American Indian Alcoholics," Alcoholism: Clinical and Experimental Research 1984, March-April vol 8(2) 179-184.

Thirty-seven male and eight female American Indian alcoholics were intensively studied in 1970-1971.   In addition to the usual demographic characteristics, alcoholism history, Indian culture affiliation scale, social competence scale, legal and psychiatric problems, and physical illnesses were assessed.   These findings in 1970-1971 were then correlated with a four-item outcome rating obtained in 1980-1981. Better outcome was associated with less parental loss, never having been married, compliance with treatment recommendations, and having predominantly Indian rather than Non-indian friends. Female SS were unlikely to deteriorate and still survive, although this was the most frequent pattern among males. Higher Indian culture affiliation and more severe liver dysfunction in 1970-1971 were correlated with better outcome in 1980-1981. (28 Ref.).

Wintemute, Ginger, ed.; Messer, Bonnie, ed. <u>Social Work Practice with Native American Families</u>: A Handbook. Administration for Children, Youth, and Families, 1980 Washington, D.C.

A handbook on social work practice with Native American families, developed for use by students in undergraduate social work programs and by social service practitioners who work with Native American people, is divided into four sections. The first section contains four articles, written by Joseph A. Dudley (Methodist minister and Yankton Sioux) and David Mathieu (Assistant Professor of American Indian Studies, Dakota Wesleyan University), which focus on culture, alcoholism, aging, and community-agency relationships. The second section gives six brief case illustrations depicting incidents in the daily experience of social work practitioners in agencies serving native American communities. The case illustrations describe situations of interaction between Indian people and social workers, then give discussion questions and a conclusion which clarifies the cultural influences shaping the situation. The third section provides an annotated bibliography of 21 books and articles helpful in social work teaching and curriculum planning for practice with native American people, and lists 4 sources of case studies. The fourth section lists tribal headquarters in South Dakota, including those of the Cheyenne River Sioux, Crow Creek Sioux, Flandreau Santee Sioux, Lower Brule Sioux, Oglala Sioux, Rosbud Sioux, Siggeton-Wahpeton Sioux, Standing Rock Sioux, and Yankton Sioux Tribes.

Wolin, S.J. "Family Culture, Family Conflicts and Family Therapy," Conference Paper. 1981 Annual School on Alcohol and Addiction Studies. Anchorage, AK: 4-7, May, 1981. 345 p. (pp. 117-166).

Comments and questions by workshop participants concerning family dynamics and marital interaction are addressed in relation to culture and cultural variables, such as values and shared belief systems.

An attempt is made to demonstrate that by focusing on these issues, therapists will be better able to work with alcoholic couples.

URBAN VS. RURAL

Alameda County Task Force on Youth and Alcohol Report
on Student Alcohol Use. <u>Alameda County, California:</u>
<u>Alameda County Task Force on Youth and Alcohol</u>, 1980.

Results from a survey conducted during January through
March, 1980, on the use of alcohol by students in
Alameda County (California) schools are presented.
Overall, 20 schools county-wide participated in this
survey as a representative sample of the entire county.
It was found that: (1) 15.7 percent of the students
reported frequent use (50 or more times) of alcohol in
the past year; (2) 1.8 percent of the students reported
having an actual drinking problem (county wide estimate
of problem drinkers was between 899 and 1293; (3) beer
was the most popular beverage overall among moderate
and frequent drinkers, and among ethnic groups and
grade levels; (4) 62 percent of the ninth graders
reported drinking beer in the past year (6.7 percent of
these reported frequent use), and 74.0 percent of the
twelfth graders reported drinking beer in the past year
(20.6 percent of these reported frequent use; (5)
overall, 9.7 percent of the students reported "getting
really drunk" more than 10 times in the past year; (6)
females generally reported lower frequent usage levels
than males, but exhibited similar drinking patterns
when comparing occasional (one to nine times) and
moderate use (10-49 times); (7) Native Americans and
Whites reported the highest frequent usage (first and
second) with Hispanics reporting a close third, while
Blacks and Asians were a full 12-13 percent below
Hispanics in terms of frequent use; (8) 83 percent of
the students felt that they knew enough about the
effects of alcohol, while 57 percent felt that more
alcohol education was needed in their schools; and (9)
students comments regarding alcohol were split between
those who felt that more help was needed and that
alcohol was a problem, and those who felt it was okay

in moderation, that kids drank just for fun, and that it was not a serious problem at all. A copy of the survey form is appended.

Bittker, Thomas E. "Dilemmas of Mental Health Service Delivery to Off-Reservation Indians," Anthropological Quarterly, 46, 1973, pp. 172-182.

Southwest Indians from the Phoenix catchment region are the subjects of this article which points out their ambiguous status once they leave the reservation mental health program. The general population are not aware of Indians and ore often feel no responsibility as they are considered to be wards of the government. At the same time the government considers them to be outside the scope of federal programs which are reservation based. Their need for services is evident in increased rates of arrests, alcoholism and alcohol related illnesses and deaths, suicide attempts and other socioemotional disorders. Indian health service attempts to fill the gap are thwarted by understaffed and inadequately funded programs dictated by a rapidly emerging federal policy to deemphasize the delivery of direct services to all the population--white or Indian. The author recommends comprehensive efforts to remedy the overall socioeconomic conditions which underlie most mental problems rather than piecemeal efforts aimed at assimilating the American Indian into the larger dominant culture. A caution is offered to approach Indian problems with sensitivity to the needs of various cultural groups among the off-reservation Indian communities and with a willingness to invite each of these groups into participation with Indian oriented programs.

Brelsford, Gregg "Athabascan Drinking Behavior: A Preliminary Ethnography" Alaska Department of Health and Social Services Quarterly Magazine, 34, 1977, pp. 14-20.

Social aspects of drinking behavior in a rural Athabascan village in Alaska are described, including systemic patterns of drinking, the implicit rules and values which prescribe alcohol consumption, the frequency and duration of individual drinking activity, the role of the young, and the effects of drinking. The system of drinking behavior is supported by economic, social, and religious factors, which together constitute the cultural dimension of drinking which must be acknowledged by alcohol rehabilitation programs. Information was gathered by a mental health worker during 1974-1975 in an isolated Athabascan village of 270 people. Because the village is legally dry and there are no commercial liquor outlets nearby,

alcohol arrives almost exclusively on the small planes
that serve the village. Drinking is intense when it
occurs but the duration is irregular.

Cockerham, William C.   "Patterns of Alcohol and
Multiple Drug Use Among Rural White and American Indian
Adolescents," International Journal of the Addictions,
12(2-z-3): 271-285, 1977.

A survey was conducted to determine attitudes and
practices concerning alcohol and other drug use among
samples of rural white and rural American Indian
adolescents. The findings showed that both groups
approved of drinking, but that the Indians tended to
get drunk more often and to approve the use of drugs
other than alcohol. Among drinkers only, the Indians
were more likely that the Whites to have smoked
marijuana. Among nondrinkers only, the Whites were
more likely than the Indians to have not tried hard
drugs. The data seems to suggest that, at the present
time, rural American Indian youth are more prone that
rural white youth to be involved with alcohol,
marijuana, and hard drugs. 28 Ref.

Hahn, D. B.   "Statewide Comparison of Student Alcohol
and Marijuana Use Patterns at Urban and Rural Public
Schools," Journal of School Health 52(4): 250-255,
1982.

A study was conducted to compare differences in alcohol
and marijuana use between urban and rural seventh,
ninth, tenth, and twelfth grade students (N=11,277).
Through the collection and analysis of this data, it
was anticipated that an accurate picture of use and
abuse of these drugs would be provided for purposes of
public debate and policy-making. Significantly more
students in the urban sample reported that they used
alcohol than students in the urban sample. Among the
urban students, 27 percent of the seventh graders, 54
percent of the ninth graders, 61 percent of the tenth
graders, and 69 percent of the twelfth graders reported
that they drink alcohol. Sixty-nine percent of the
twelfth graders reported that they drink alcohol.
However, 31 percent of the rural seventh grades, 62
percent of the rural ninth graders, 69 percent of the
rural tenth graders, and 78 percent of the rural
twelfth graders reported that they drink alcoholic
beverages. Findings are also reported on age of first
use and quantity and frequency of alcohol and marijuana
use. The implications of the findings are briefly
discussed, and it is concluded here that the previously
reported gulf between urban and rural student alcohol
and marijuana use may no longer exist. 9 Ref.

Hill, T. W.   "Life Styles and Drinking Patterns of Urban Indians"   Journal of Drug Issues, 10(2):   257-272, 1980.

The major life styles and drinking patterns of the "everyday" Winnebago and Santee Dakota of Sioux City, Iowa, are described.   An intensive research   strategy and methodology which included extensive participant observation were used in the collection of data. Throughout the research an attempt was made to see drinking activities in terms of the Indians' cultural systems.   In contrast to the researchers who argue that a single set of drinking standards or norms is shared across ethnic and class lines in the United States, it is shown that multiple sets are used by the Indians of Sioux City and that some sets define some forms of heavy and frequent drinking as acceptable behavior.   51 Ref.

Jackson, N.: Carlisi, J.: Greenway, C.: Zalesnick, M. "Age of Initial Drug Experimentation Among White and Non-White Ethnics,"   International Journal of the Addictions,   16(8) :   1373-1386, 1981.

A 196 item questionnaire on ethnic background and drug use patterns was administered to 1414 students in inner city communities of Baltimore, Detroit, Cincinnati, and Providence.   The students were asked to report the age at which they first tried cigarettes, inhalants, alcohol, marijuana, barbiturates, codeine, methadone, cocaine, hallucinogens, amphetamines, Valium, and heroin.   Results revealed significant differences in actual age of experimentation among ethnic groups, as well as differences in other general patterns relating to age of first drug use.   A comparison of Whites to non-Whites showed little difference in ages of initial drug experimentation.   Polish, Italian, German, and black youth tended to try most drugs at a later age than average, whereas native Americans and mixed Race youth (those whose parents were of different races) tended to try drugs at an earlier age.   25 Ref.

Miller, M.; Wittstock, L.W. "American Indian Alcoholism in St. Paul."   Minneapolis, Mn.:   Center for Urban and Regional Affairs, 1981, 60 p.

A needs assessment survey concerning American Indian alcoholism in St. Paul, Minnesota, was conducted jointly by the Community Planning Organization and the Juel Fairbanks Aftercare Residence, a halfway house facility primarily serving American Indians in St. Paul/Ramsey County.   An overview of the Indian population and the Indian alcoholism problem in Minnesota, in general, and St. Paul, in particular,   is   provided.

Results are presented from a survey (1980) designed to determine what is effective with Indian clients in terms of treatment techniques, treatment environments, and factors in maintaining sobriety following treatment. Recommendations for appropriate changes in alcoholism services and treatment programs for Indians are enumerated. Survey data and comments are appended, and an annotated bibliography is provided.

Phillips, P.; Phin, J.G. "Drug Treatment Entry Patterns and Socioeconomic Characteristics of Asian American, Native American, and Puerto Rican Clients." In: A.J. Schecter, Ed., Drug Dependence & Alcoholism, Vol. 2: Social & Behavioral Issues. New York, NY: Plenum Press, 1981. 1041 p. (pp. 803-818).

The first report is presented form a four-part study describing the nature and extent of drug (including alcohol) abuse problems and effective treatment for minorities. Minority treatment in those five cities with the largest in-treatment concentrations of Asian Americans, Native Americans, and Puerto Ricans is examined. Treatment process and outcome are related to cultural issues, and implications for alterations in the current delivery system are highlighted. Since the design could not account for national patterns, minority-specific findings from the National Institute on Drug Abuse Client Oriented Data Acquisition Process (CODAP) system are included within each discussion as a reference for comparison. 3 Ref.

Turner, E. "Medicine Wheel: An Approach to Treatment," Conference paper. 1981 Annual School on Alcohol and Addiction Studies, Anchorage, AK: 4-7, May 1981. 345 p. (pp. 233-265).

The philosophy and some approaches of the Seattle (Washington) Indian Alcoholism Program are described. It is noted that: (1) while the incidence of physical addiction to alcohol among Indians and non-Indians is comparable, the incidence of psychological addiction to alcohol is three to four times greater among Indians than among non-Indians; (2) four out of the top causes of death among Indians are alcohol-related, with alcohol being the number one cause of accidents; (3) of all Indian arrests and deaths, 90 percent and 32 percent are alcohol-related, respectively; and (4) binge drinking is the most common consumption pattern among Indians, with group drinking and binge drinking the most popular forms, as opposed to daily alcohol consumption. Comments and questions by workshop participants are addressed.

United States. American Indian Policy Review

Commission.   Task Force 8.   Report on Urban and Rural
Non-Reservation Indians.   Final Report to The American
Indian Policy Review Commission.   Washington, D.C.:
Congress of the United States, Government Printing
Office, 1976, 147 p.

The result of a 12-month investigation of rural and
urban nonreservation American Indian needs.   This
report is the final produce of a task force assigned by
the American Indian Policy Review Commission to: (1)
Examine statutes and procedures for granting federal
recognition and extending services to American Indians;
(2) Collect and compile data re: The extent of present
and projected Indian needs; (3) Explore the feasibility
of alternative elective bodies to facilitate maximum
decision making participation.   Included in this report
are: the   executive   summary   of   findings   and
recommendations; task force methodology (contact with
167 urban Indian organizations, 12 regional hearings,
and a need classification including 18 broad subject
areas); an historical review of the Indian and federal
government relationship; a legal review (emphasis on
authorizing services to nonreservation Indians); a
social needs assessment (employment; education;
housing; health; frequently mentioned need areas --
legal services; adoption, elderly care, alcoholism
counseling; facilities, transportation; the Indian
Center; rural nonreservation; and Indian poverty levels
and income characteristics); exploration of alternative
elective bodies (an independent Indian agency to manage
federal funding and services and council of off-
reservation advisors for the Bureau of Indian Affairs
and the Indian Health Service).

Waddell, J.O. "From Tank to Townshouse: Probing the
Impact of a Legal Reform on the Drinking Styles of
Urban Papago Indians."   Urban Anthropology, 5(2): 187-
198, 1976.

The impact of an Arizona intoxication code on the
traditional drinking styles of Papago Indians in the
urban setting of Tucson, Arizona is assessed.
Historical practices of city handling of Indian drunks
are briefly reviewed, including those in effect as late
as 1970, when a comprehensive field study on urban
Papago drinking was undertaken.   The radical change in
administering public intoxication cases is evaluated in
light of its impact on the urban Papagos.   This change
was brought about by a public law that no longer
allowed municipal governments the right to arrest, try,
convict, and sentence to jail public drunks, but which
required, instead, the establishment of local reception
centers for detoxification, counseling, and referral.
Preliminary conclusions regarding the impact of

institutional change on urban Papago Indian drinking are presented.   7 Ref.

Walker, R.D. "Treatment Strategies in an Urban Indian Alcoholism Program," Journal of Studies on Alcohol, Suppl. No. 9: 171-184, 1981.

The development of the Seattle (Washington) Indian Alcoholism Program (SIAP) is briefly described, and the relationship between SIAP treatment approaches and treatment outcome is examined.   This program was established by the local Seattle Indian community and is recognized by both Indian and non-Indian community alcoholism treatment agencies as a successful program. SIAP represents a social model for the treatment of alcoholism, whose approach is multimodal and, to some degree, multidisciplinary.   Characteristics of 72 clients in SIAP from January to July 1978 are also described, and Alcohol Use Inventory scores of these clients are compared to those of 1,030 alcoholics at Fort Logan Mental Health Center (Colorado).   Because of differences in drinking patterns among Indian groups and the types of psychosocial situations in which they exist, no single therapeutic modality is suitable in all Indian treatment programs.   Posthospital aftercare follow-up appears to facilitate reentry of clients into their communities.   The success SIAP has had in identifying clients and engaging them in treatment is a first step in addressing this serious problem of American Indians. 19 Ref.

Weibel, J. C. " American Indians, Urbanization, and Alcohol: A Developing Urban Indian Drinking Ethos," Alcohol and Health Monograph No. 4: Special Population Issues, Rockville, MD.: National Institute on Alcohol Abuse and Alcoholism, 1982, pp. 331-358.

Research studies on the urbanization of American Indians are cited and discussed. The use of alcohol by Indians in urban environments as a coping strategy is described. Studies of Los Angeles (California)

Weibel, J. "There's a Place for Everything and Everything in its Place: Environmental Influences on Urban Indian Drinking Patterns." In: T.C. Harford and L.S. Gaines, Eds., Social Drinking Contexts. Washington, DC: 17-19, Sep, 1979. 244 p. (pp. 206-227).

Elements of social context are analyzed.   Six environmental dimensions are identified, their associated drinking levels and drinking styles are examined. These dimensions are applied to four urban Indian settings; Fifth Sunday Sing, Saturday night powwows, ruralized weekend powwows, and urban Indian

bars.   Based upon participant observations in a wide
range of drinking and nondrinking settings, this study
shows that Indians have no single drinking style, but
seem to shift their drinking behavior across settings.
The hypothesis is explored that specific qualities or
dimensions of a setting may either mitigate or increase
drinking behavior, and that individuals respond to such
environmental cues diversely according to their
cultural backgrounds and lifestyles.   21 Ref.

Weibel, J. C.   "American Indians, Urbanization, and
Alcohol: A Developing Urban Indian Drinking Ethos."
In: Alcohol and Health Monograph No.4: Special
Population Issues. Rockville, Md.:   National Institute
on Alcohol Abuse and Alcoholism, pp. 331-358, 1982.

Research studies on the urbanization of American
Indians are cited and discussed.   The use of alcohol by
Indians in urban environments as a coping strategy is
described.   Studies of Los Angeles (California) Indian
drinking practices are summarized as exemplars of urban
Indian alcohol abuse issues.   An Indian versus national
alcohol consumption profile is presented, and cultural
and contextual influences on Indian drinking levels are
discussed.   Differences in drinking patterns between
rural and urban Indians are briefly described, and
recommendations for future research associated with
alcohol abuse among urban Indians are provided.   It is
concluded that these research areas need immediate
attention by social and biological scientists if
culturally viable treatment modalities for the Indian
alcohol abuser are to be developed.   118 Ref.

Weibel-Orlando, J., Weisner, T., Long, J.   "Urban and
Rural Indian Drinking Patterns: Implications for
Intervention   Policy   Development,"   Substance and
Alcohol Actions/Misuse, 5(1):   45-57, 1984.

The drinking patterns and alcohol consumption level
differences between urban and rural Indians in
California are compared to gain insight into the causes
of alcohol misuse among Native Americans and to
establish effective prevention and treatment measures.
In both rural and urban areas, the average level of
beer drinking is higher for males than for females.
The increase from adolescent drinking levels to young
adult drinking levels is somewhat greater in urban
drinkers than among their rural counterparts.   Urban
Indian males tend to drink more frequently than their
rural counterparts, while there is a leveling off of
drinking with increased age in rural areas.   The urban
social milieu is more conducive to chronically heavy
drinking than the rural social milieu where there is
more exposure to relatives and friends.   It is

recommended that accelerated prevention, as well as recovery programs, be initiated in rural Indian communities as they have been among the urban male Indian populations. It is suggested that increased intervention emphasis be directed to at risk populations, in particular, adolescent and post adolescent members of Indian communities and Indian females who consume large amounts of alcohol with regularity. It is concluded that Indian alcohol intervention programs which involve family, friends, and members of the client's support network in the recovery process be implemented. 73 Ref.

Winfree, L., Thomas; Griffiths, Curt T., Theis, Harold E. "Drug, Ethnicity and the Impact of Social Control Mechanisms: Drug Use in a Rural School System". Paper. Sociological Abstracts, 1978.

An investigation was conducted to determine the amount of drug use among children in a rural area with a sizable minority population. Data were collected in 1975 from students, grades 6-12, in a western mountain state. The study was concerned with: Formal and informal mechanisms; and Native American and Caucasian perceptions of those mechanisms. The results show preference for informal control mechanisms over formal mechanisms in explaining usage patterns. A difference is found in drug use patterns between Native Americans and Caucasians. 17.2 percent of the sample were Native Americans.

SUBJECT INDEX

AUTHOR INDEX

About the Authors

MICHAEL L. LOBB is an Assistant Professor in the Graduate School of Social Work at the University of Texas at Arlington. He is the author of many scholarly papers and has contributed articles to the *Bulletin of the Psychonomic Society, Animal Learning and Behavior,* and *Child Welfare.*

THOMAS D. WATTS is a Professor in the Graduate School of Social Work at the University of Texas at Arlington. His earlier works include *The Societal Learning Approach: A New Approach to Social Welfare Policy and Planning in America,* and his essays, book chapters, journal articles, and book reviews have been widely published in professional journals, collections, and monographs.